TAKE ONE VEG

GEORGINA FUGGLE is a young chef and food stylist who has trained at Leith's, worked for Green & Black's and been a Senior Food Editor. She grew up helping her father with his vegetable patch and now runs several pop-up restaurants called Hart & Fuggle with her friend Alice Hart. Her first book for Kyle Books was *Take One Pot*. Her blog is fuggleantics.blogspot.com.

TAKE ONE VEG

OVER 100 TEMPTING VEGGIE RECIPES FOR
SIMPLE SUPPERS, PACKED LUNCHES AND
WEEKEND COOKING

Georgina Fuggle

PHOTOGRAPHY BY TORI HANCOCK

KYLE BOOKS LTD

First published in Great Britain in 2015 by
Kyle Books, an imprint of Kyle Cathie Ltd
192–198 Vauxhall Bridge Road
London SW1V 1DX
general.enquiries@kylebooks.com
www.kylebooks.com

10 9 8 7 6 5 4 3 2 1

ISBN 978 0 85783 233 7

If you are vegetarian, please use vegetarian-friendly,
alternative cheeses for Parmesan, pecorino and Gorgonzola.

Designer: Nicky Collings
Photographer: Tori Hancock
Food Stylist: Georgina Fuggle
Prop Stylist: Liz Belton
Project Editor: Sophie Allen
Copy Editor: Emma Clegg
Editorial Assistant: Claire Rogers
Production: Nic Jones, Gemma John and Lisa Pinnell

A Cataloguing in Publication record for this title is available
from the British Library.

Colour reproduction by ALTA London
Printed and bound in China by 1010 International
Printing Ltd

CONTENTS

INTRODUCTION

Vegetarian cookery has transformed in the last few years. Cooks are experimenting with vegetables, being braver with their texture, brilliant colour and variety of flavour. In today's cuisine culture, meat is not the only expected master of the main course and diners are more than content to see the once humble vegetable catapulted into the limelight.

Vegetables are cost effective, nutritious and obliging to a novice cook. They sit without spoiling, are forgiving to a touch too much spice (or seasoning) and, importantly, accommodate a slightly smaller budget. Quite aside from our own desires, it just isn't sustainable for us to continue to eat the amount of meat that we are, and serving it will become a luxury that many of us simply aren't able to indulge. So sit up, take heed and learn to cook creatively with vegetables.

Don't be scared to try new recipes, add layers with extra garlic or fresh herbs and try new exciting varieties. Allow delicate flavours to marry with each other, forming trusted relationships such as the dependable friendship of potato and onion, or more unusual partnerships such as tenderstem broccoli and hot red chilli. Present your food to the table with poise knowing there is nothing, nothing more delicious than a recipe that has been cooked with effort and care.

My parents taught me about vegetables, about dedicating a patch at the end of the garden to growth, vitality and being experimental about planting. If beans don't succeed one year, change the variety or try something new. Yes, supermarkets sell all of the vegetables mentioned here, but if time allows, take a moment to visit a local farm shop or market. The varieties will almost certainly be more adventurous and the flavour far superior to those bred for the shelves of the mass market. Your cooking is also more likely to reflect the seasons, which is always a good thing.

The chapters are divided into clusters of vegetable varieties, loosely based on the scientific families. There are nine major groups ranging from the strident Brassicaceae (all things cabbage-like) to the Cucurbitaceae (an umbrella term for the marrow clan). There are some anomalies within the chapters, such as the sweetcorn and radishes in Beans and Summer Greens, but I've grouped the veg where I feel they fit best for their cooking qualities and seasonality. Each recipe has a 'star of the show', a lead vegetable that the other ingredients will follow. Some will feel very familiar – the cosy recognisable carrot – while others may not, such as the lime green Romanesco cauliflower.

I've included an array of recipes – big, wholesome winter warmers, light, healthy summer salads, nourishing grains perfect for a weeknight supper or packed lunch and a few sweets to suit occasions throughout the year – all are simple to make and satisfying to eat. Many of them are inherited, rather than developed and many were served to me as a child before I served them to my own family. I hope you enjoy my collection.

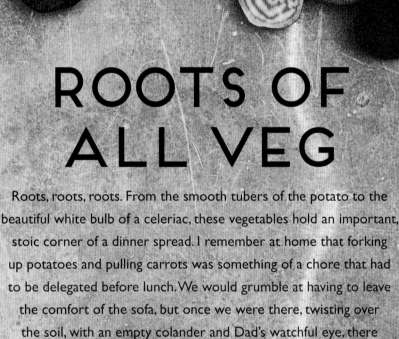

ROOTS OF ALL VEG

Roots, roots, roots. From the smooth tubers of the potato to the
beautiful white bulb of a celeriac, these vegetables hold an important,
stoic corner of a dinner spread. I remember at home that forking
up potatoes and pulling carrots was something of a chore that had
to be delegated before lunch. We would grumble at having to leave
the comfort of the sofa, but once we were there, twisting over
the soil, with an empty colander and Dad's watchful eye, there
was something prehistorically exciting and immensely
satisfying about turning over earth
to reveal edible treats.

JERUSALEM ARTICHOKE

FARRO AND HAZELNUT SALAD

I've noticed in recent years that farro has become the darling grain of many restaurants. It has a beautiful nutty flavour and becomes tender quickly but avoids turning mushy. It is ideal for a warm salad with a sharp oily dressing and soft, rich artichoke topped with poached egg.

SERVES 4 – PREP TIME: 20 MINUTES
COOK TIME: 40 MINUTES

200g semi pearled farro
500g Jerusalem artichokes, scrubbed clean but not
    peeled, each cut in quarters
2 tablespoons olive oil
50g baby spinach leaves
1 small red onion, finely sliced
50g hazelnuts, toasted and roughly chopped
4 medium free-range eggs
1 teaspoon red chilli flakes, for sprinkling
salt and freshly ground black pepper

For the dressing
juice of ½ lemon
2 tablespoons cider vinegar
50ml extra virgin olive oil
2 teaspoons coriander seeds, crushed with a pestle
    and mortar

1 Tip the farro into a medium saucepan and cover with 5cm of water. Bring to the boil, reduce the heat and continue to cook over a low heat for about 30 minutes until the farro is tender. Drain and set aside.

2 Meanwhile, preheat the oven to 200°C/180°C fan/gas mark 6. Place the artichokes on a roasting tray, drizzle with the olive oil and season with salt and pepper. Bake in the oven for about 30 minutes until soft and cooked through.

3 Make the dressing by combining the lemon juice, vinegar, oil and coriander seeds and pour this over the cooked farro. Stir through the spinach, red onion and 25g of the chopped hazelnuts. Finally, add the artichoke.

4 Bring a wide saucepan of water to the boil. Poach the eggs gently in the water for a couple of minutes until softly set (2 eggs at a time might be easier; see page 26 for how to poach eggs).

5 Taste and add more seasoning to the salad if necessary. Serve your farro salad warm, topped with the poached eggs, the remaining hazelnuts and a sprinkling of chilli flakes.

POTATOES
DAUPHINOISE WITH GRUYÈRE AND THYME

Creative adjustments to recipes can make interesting variations, but some recipes have no need for deviation: repetition is the only way. Here we have an absolute classic of potatoes, thyme, garlic and a healthy amount of cream – this can be eaten solo with a fresh green salad.

SERVES 8 – PREP TIME: 20 MINUTES (PLUS 10 MINUTES RESTING)
COOK TIME: 1 HOUR 40 MINUTES

300ml double cream
300ml semi-skimmed milk
3 large garlic cloves, crushed
4 sprigs of thyme, leaves picked
butter, for greasing
1kg floury potatoes, peeled and sliced into
    3–4mm slices (or as thinly as you can)

2 onions, halved and thinly sliced
40g Gruyère cheese, finely grated
salt and freshly ground black pepper

2-litre ovenproof dish

1 Preheat the oven to 180°C/160°C fan/gas mark 4. Heat the cream, milk, garlic and thyme in a small pan. Simmer for a minute or two, allowing the garlic to infuse into the cream. Remove from the heat and allow to cool completely.

2 Meanwhile, adjust the oven to 200°C/180°C fan/gas mark 6 and place a baking tray on the centre shelf.

3 Butter the ovenproof dish. Layer up the sliced potato and onion on the bottom of the dish. Season well, then continue to layer until all the potato slices and onion have been used. Slowly pour over the garlicky cream mixture, allowing each addition to find the crevices and become absorbed before adding more. Season again.

4 Sprinkle over the Gruyère and a few more thyme leaves. Bake for between 1 hour 20 minutes and 1 hour 30 minutes or until the potato cuts like butter.

5 Allow the Dauphinoise potatoes to sit for a good 10 minutes before serving – this allows them to settle down and results in a better tasting dish.

tip! *The oven needs to be really hot and up to temperature before you put the potatoes in, which is why you preheat the oven at 180°C before increasing to 200°C.*

HASSELBACK
POTATOES
WITH ROSEMARY

Potatoes are an unbeatable year-round food — comforting, modest, easy coming and easy going. If you would like a change from familiar potato recipes, try this for an easy but striking dish. One tip to remember is that the thinner the potatoes, the crispier they become.

SERVES 8 – PREP TIME: 20 MINUTES
COOK TIME: 1 HOUR 10 MINUTES

40g butter, melted
3 tablespoons extra virgin olive oil
8–10 large floury potatoes
2 small onions, cut into wedges
sea salt for seasoning

2 stems of rosemary
salt and freshly ground
black pepper

22cm ovenproof dish

1 Preheat the oven to 200°C/180°C fan/gas mark 6. Combine the melted butter with the oil and use some to liberally brush the ovenproof dish.

2 Keeping the skins on, slice the potatoes as thinly as possible, but avoid cutting them all the way to the base. A good tip is to place a skewer on the surface next to the potato and slice down onto that so the knife will be prevented from cutting all the way through.

3 Put the potatoes in the prepared dish and nestle the onion wedges around them. Douse the dish in most of the remaining butter and oil mixture, aiming to get some inside the potato slices. Season generously with salt.

4 Cook the potatoes in the oven for 50 minutes. Then remove and brush them with the remaining butter and oil. Scatter over the leaves from the rosemary and season well with salt and pepper. Return to the oven for a final 20 minutes, or until the potatoes are cooked through and crispy on the outside.

POTATO

My brother James says the mark of a real cook is someone who cooks a curry from scratch. A home-cooked version does require a well stocked spice rack but once you've got that up and running there is no excuse to revert to the supermarket versions. One tip is to make the curry an hour or two before it's needed and simply reheat; the flavour will only deepen and intensify.

SERVES 6 – PREP TIME: 20 MINUTES
COOK TIME: 40 MINUTES

10 medium waxy potatoes, cut into
 bite-size chunks
2 tablespoons olive oil
2 teaspoons mustard seeds
1 teaspoon fennel seeds
2 medium onions, roughly chopped
1 teaspoon ground coriander
1 teaspoon red chilli powder
1 teaspoon turmeric powder
1 teaspoon garam masala

1 large red chilli (or small if you like it hotter),
 deseeded and finely sliced
a handful of coriander leaves, to garnish
salt and freshly ground black pepper

For the tomato sauce
4 large tomatoes
7cm piece of fresh ginger, peeled and
 roughly chopped
1 tablespoon tomato purée
8 garlic cloves

1 Put the potatoes in a large saucepan and cover them with cold water. Bring to the boil over a medium heat and simmer for 12–14 minutes or until the potatoes are tender and can easily be cut through with a knife.

2 Prepare the tomato sauce. Deseed the tomatoes by cutting each in half, scooping out the watery seeds (a dessertspoon is the best tool for this job) and roughly chop. Put the tomato flesh, ginger, tomato purée and garlic in a small blender or food-processor and whizz until you have a bright, fresh sauce.

3 Heat the olive oil in a large, deep frying pan over a medium heat. Add the mustard seeds and fennel seeds and fry for 1–2 minutes until the seeds just begin to pop. Add the onion and continue to fry for 3–4 minutes until softened and slightly golden in colour. Add the coriander, chilli powder, turmeric, garam masala and red chilli.

4 Stir the potatoes through the beautiful spice mix and continue to cook for 2–3 minutes.

5 Pour the fresh tomato and ginger sauce into the potatoes and simmer for 15–20 minutes until the sauce and the potatoes have become well acquainted. Season and serve, garnished with fresh coriander.

SUNSHINE POTATO

SALAD

Here we have a smarter, more sophisticated and lighter version of the well rehearsed potato salad. The combination of soured cream, lemon and mayonnaise make up the base of the dressing, with the capers and dill providing plenty of flavour. Serve at almost any occasion when the weather is warm and new potatoes are in season.

SERVES 4 – PREP TIME: 25 MINUTES
COOK TIME: 15 MINUTES

500g baby new potatoes
juice and zest of 2 unwaxed lemons
125ml soured cream
2 tablespoons mayonnaise
½ teaspoon mustard powder
½ red onion, finely diced

2 tablespoons baby capers, roughly chopped
4 tablespoons finely chopped dill fronds,
   plus extra to garnish
80g fresh pea shoots
salt and freshly ground black pepper

1 Cut any larger potatoes in half and place in a medium sized saucepan of cold water. Bring to the boil and simmer for 10–12 minutes until tender. Drain and tip into a large bowl. Allow to cool for a few minutes.

2 Add the lemon juice and and zest and dollop in the soured cream and mayonnaise. Mix well. Add the mustard powder, red onion, capers and dill and gently mix the ingredients together. Season with salt and black pepper.

3 Gently toss the potato salad with the bright green pea shoots. Garnish with plenty of black pepper and an extra scattering of dill fronds.

SWEET POTATO

AND GOAT'S CHEESE TRIANGLES

Raw, boiled, roasted, baked or stuffed, the sweet potato is one of autumn's most welcome pleasures. Here it sits with roasted aubergine and soft goat's cheese, all encased in a crisp filo triangle.

MAKES 6 LARGE TRIANGLES – PREP TIME: 35 MINUTES
COOK TIME: 45 MINUTES

500g sweet potatoes, peeled and chopped into
   2–3cm cubes
1 teaspoon smoked paprika
1 tablespoon olive oil, plus extra for brushing
1 large aubergine (around 300g), sliced into
   20–24 thin slices, each 5mm in diameter
½ × 400g can chickpeas (drained weight 125g)
zest of 1 unwaxed lemon

For the parcels
3 sheets of filo, measuring a minimum of
   40 × 15cm
50g butter, melted
100g soft goat's cheese, cut into 6 generous rounds

1 Preheat the oven to 200°C/180°C fan/gas mark 6. Put the sweet potato into a roasting tin in an even layer and sprinkle with the smoked paprika and a healthy drizzle of olive oil. Roast for 20 minutes until just tender (roasting them is a good method of retaining the flavour while also extracting some of the extra moisture).

2 Brush each aubergine slice with a little olive oil on both sides and fry over a high heat until the sides have curled and each slice is cooked through. Set aside.

3 Remove the sweet potato from the oven and put it into a bowl. Using a potato masher, mash until the cubes have all but disappeared and stir though the chickpeas and lemon zest.

tip! *If the filo you buy is not quite long enough, then simply join two sheets together and secure with melted butter.*

4 Cut the filo sheets in half horizontally to create two long lengths of pastry and brush the pastry all over with melted butter. Cover the remaining pastry with a damp tea-towel to keep fresh.

5 Put one-sixth of the sweet potato mixture on the sheet of pastry. Top with 3–4 rounds of aubergine and a round of goat's cheese. Fold the bottom corner up to meet the top side to start the shape of a triangle. Fold the bottom point of the pastry up, sealing in the filling, then complete the triangle by folding again in the opposite direction. Keep folding until you reach the top and lightly brush with more melted butter. Repeat until you have finished the filling.

6 Place the triangles on a baking tray and cook for 20 minutes, until golden.

SWEET POTATO
GNOCCHI IN HOT SAGE BUTTER

These sweet, soft pillows are a joy to make and far easier than you might imagine. A plateful will sit as happily at a children's teatime as it does at an adult dinner party.

SERVES 4 – PREP TIME: 30 MINUTES
COOK TIME: 30 MINUTES

1 large potato (around 400g)
1 large sweet potato (around 400g)
200g strong bread flour
1 medium free-range egg yolk
½ teaspoon salt and a pinch of black pepper

flour, for dusting
bowl of iced water
50g unsalted butter
5 sage leaves, finely chopped
Parmesan cheese, to serve

1 Peel and cut both varieties of potato into 2–3cm chunks, cutting the sweet potato slightly larger than the standard potato to ensure they both steam at the same rate. Put them in a steamer and steam for about 20 minutes until the flesh cuts like butter – this is the most effective cooking method as very little water is absorbed.

2 Allow the potatoes to cool slightly before mashing them well. Sift the flour over the surface of the cooled potato and mix it in. Add the egg yolk, salt and pepper and continue to mix until you have a soft dough. Add a little more flour if necessary, but stop as soon as the mixture comes together.

3 Set the dough aside while you clean the work surface and dust it with flour. Roughly divide the dough into 3 pieces and roll each piece into a long sausage shape. Chop the dough into 3cm pieces with a floured knife. Put the finished gnocchi on a flour-dusted tray.

4 Bring a large pan of salted water to the boil, then turn down to a simmer, and tip in half the gnocchi. Stir and wait for them to rise to the surface after about 2–3 minutes. This means the gnocchi is cooked. Remove them with a slotted spoon and immediately place in a bowl of iced water to stop the cooking process. Repeat with the remaining gnocchi.

5 Heat the butter in a large frying pan and add the chopped sage. Fry for a minute or two before tipping in the cooked gnocchi. Coat the gnocchi in the beautiful herby butter, grate over some Parmesan and transfer to serving plates. Eat immediately, with a good pinch of salt.

tip! *If you cut the gnocchi evenly they will cook evenly.*

SWEET POTATO

STUFFED WITH BUTTER BEANS, GREENS AND BLACK OLIVES

God's gift to potatoes was to make a sweet variety that still sits neatly within the 'healthy' camp. They are often eaten in our house dressed simply with salted butter, but this recipe creates a quick, fresh filling that elevates this dish into one that's perfect for entertaining.

SERVES 4 – PREP TIME: 15 MINUTES
COOK TIME: 50 MINUTES

4 large sweet potatoes, scrubbed clean
olive oil, for rubbing the potatoes
40g butter
2 large garlic cloves, crushed
pinch of dried chilli flakes
75g black olives

1 × 400g can butter beans, drained and rinsed
150g spring greens, sliced into thin strips
juice and zest of 1 large unwaxed lemon
salt and freshly ground black pepper
crème fraîche, to serve

1 Preheat the oven to 180°C/160°C fan/gas mark 4. Rub the potatoes with a little oil, put on a baking tray and cook for 45–50 minutes until the skins have slightly puffed up and the orange flesh is tender.

2 Roughly 15 minutes before your sweet potatoes are ready, start on the filling. Melt the butter in a high-sided frying pan (or shallow lidded saucepan), add the garlic and chilli flakes and fry over a medium heat until the garlic smells cooked, for about 1–2 minutes. Add the olives and butter beans to the pan and stir to combine. Finally, stir through the shredded greens. Cover with a lid and cook, stirring occasionally, for 5–6 minutes.

3 Remove the lid, season well, squeeze over the fresh lemon juice and stir through the lemon zest.

4 Cut the cooked sweet potatoes in half lengthways and pinch each end to create a boat. Stuff with the lemony, buttery greens. Season and serve with a dollop of crème fraîche.

BUTTERY MASHED
SWEDE
WITH SAGE

Americans call the swede rutabaga. The Scots call it neeps. Whichever name you use, the vegetable is the same: glorious purple-green with sweet orange flesh, ideal for steaming, mashing or roasting. My family have always completed a roast with mashed swede sitting alongside the roasted potatoes – to this day, I never think a roast dinner is complete without it.

SERVES 4 AS A SIDE – PREP TIME: 12 MINUTES
COOK TIME: 25 MINUTES

1 large swede, peeled and chopped into chunks
50g salted butter, cubed

10–12 sage leaves, roughly chopped
sea salt and freshly ground black pepper

1 Bring a large saucepan of salted water to the boil and, once simmering, add the swede. Simmer the swede for 20 minutes until very tender. Drain well in a colander and transfer to a blender or food-processor. Pulse to a mash, but be cautious not to overdo it – you don't want a baby food consistency.

2 Return the swede mixture to a bowl and beat in 30g of the butter – the residual heat should gently melt it. Season well with sea salt and black pepper.

3 Heat the remaining butter in a small saucepan. Once hot, throw in the sage leaves and fry until they are crispy and their colour has changed to a dark earthy green. Gently spoon the sage leaves and their butter over the mash. Serve.

RAW
SWEET POTATO
GINGER AND APPLE SALAD

Sweet potato is full of antioxidants and fibre and, teamed with ginger and apple, makes this salad into a tangible health kick. Cut the sweet potato into tiny julienne strips with a tool designed for the job, but if you haven't got one use a grater.

SERVES 6 – PREP TIME: 10–15 MINUTES,
WITH FOOD-PROCESSOR – COOK TIME: 2–3 MINUTES

2 sweet potatoes (around 400g), peeled
2 crisp green apples, washed, with skin on
3 sticks celery, finely sliced
4 tablespoons roughly chopped flat-leaf parsley
50g pumpkin seeds
50g sunflower seeds

For the dressing
8cm piece of fresh ginger, peeled
juice and zest of 1 unwaxed lemon
1 teaspoon caster sugar
2 tablespoons cider vinegar
3 tablespoons extra virgin olive oil
salt and black pepper

1 This is a simple salad, but the chopping does require a little concentration. Cut the sweet potato into delicate lengths by using a julienne grater, shredding in a food-processor or grating with a coarse box grater. Do the same with the apples. Combine the potato, apple, celery and parsley in a large bowl.

2 Toast the pumpkin seeds and sunflower seeds in a frying pan over a high heat – watch them carefully as they are notoriously easy to burn!

3 For the dressing, finely grate the ginger into a small bowl or jar. Add the lemon juice and zest, the sugar, vinegar and olive oil. Add a pinch of salt and a little cracked black pepper. Mix well and pour into the sweet potato and apple mixture. Add in half the seeds and mix well. Serve, topped with the remaining toasted seeds.

tip! *If you would like to bulk this salad out a little, add a handful or two of cooked rice.*

ROOTS

I know, strictly speaking, this recipe isn't made with 'one veg', but a root vegetable medley lends itself to communal roasting. The roots are tough enough to withstand a hot oven and any caramelising only adds to their flavour. This can be a easy winter meal if you feel starved of vitamins. Alternatively you could serve it as a side to any roast.

SERVES 6 – PREP TIME: 20 MINUTES
COOK TIME: 45–50 MINUTES

1 turnip, scrubbed and cut into wedges
4 raw beetroot, peeled and cut into small wedges
3 parsnips, scrubbed and cut into quarters lengthways
6 young carrots, scrubbed clean and cut into thirds if large

3 tablespoons olive oil
a few sprigs of thyme
salt and freshly ground black pepper

1 Preheat the oven to 200°C/180°C fan/gas mark 6. Lay all the vegetables on a large ovenproof tray (use two if required). Pour over the oil and roll the vegetables about until they are all coated and glistening with oil. This can be done up to an hour in advance.

2 Add the sprigs of thyme to the vegetables and roast in the oven for 45–50 minutes until softened and beginning to caramelise. Season well and serve.

tips!
- *Spread the vegetables in a single layer – you want them to roast rather than steam.*
- *Don't flip the vegetables too often – once during cooking is generally enough.*
- *Hardy herbs – rosemary, sage and thyme – enjoy being roasted in the oven but anything more delicate – such as parsley, coriander or chives – should be added afterwards.*

variation
- *Experiment using different spices, but it is advisable to stick to one type rather than use a mixture of flavours. As a general rule a teaspoon or two is a good amount.*
- *If you don't have the vegetables listed, use whatever roots you have to hand.*

SWEDE

AND THYME ROSTI, POACHED EGGS AND HOLLANDAISE

I married into a Faroese family. The Faroe Islands lie a short flight away from Scotland, halfway between Norway and Iceland. When visiting, expect to find puffins, plenty of grass, beautiful turf roofs, soaring cliffs and endless sea views. The harsh climate dictates a diet rich in meat and fish because most vegetables aren't able to survive the lack of sun. Root vegetables, though, thrive there. This recipe takes me back to the days I spent on the islands looking for puffins, fishing and soaking up the 24 hours of daylight.

MAKES 4 ROSTI – PREP TIME: 15 MINUTES
COOK TIME: 25 MINUTES

½ swede (around 300g), peeled and cut into
    7–8cm chunks
1 medium potato (around 250g), peeled and halved
2 tablespoons thyme leaves
2 tablespoons plain flour
a large knob of butter
oil or butter, for cooking

4 medium free-range eggs
salt and freshly ground black pepper
chopped chives, to garnish

For the hollandaise sauce
2 large free-range egg yolks
1 tablespoon lemon juice
125g salted butter, cubed

1 Preheat the oven to 110°C/90°C fan/gas mark ¼. This will be used to keep the rosti and any plates warm.

2 Bring a small pan of water to the boil and add the swede and potato. Simmer for 12–14 minutes until just tender. Drain and allow to cool slightly, just enough so you can grate the vegetables without burning your fingers. Grate the swede and potatoes on the coarse side of a box grater. Gently mix the swede, potato, thyme and flour in a large bowl until well combined. Season well.

3 Heat the butter in a large frying pan. Shape the mixture into 4 patties. Fry for 3–4 minutes on each side until brown and crisp, gently pushing down the mixture as it cooks. Put the rosti onto a baking tray and into the preheated oven to keep warm.

4 To make the hollandaise sauce, set a small glass bowl over a small saucepan of simmering water and add the egg yolks, lemon juice and 1 tablespoon of cold water to the bowl. Meanwhile, melt the butter in a separate pan and

keep it warm. As the water underneath your egg yolks begins to simmer, whisk the egg yolks continuously for 3–5 minutes with a metal whisk until they are pale and fluffy. Don't stop whisking, as the mixture may otherwise curdle. Remove the bowl from the heat and, very slowly, pour in the melted butter until it is all incorporated and you are left with a creamy hollandaise. Taste and adjust the seasoning or add a little more lemon juice if needed.

5 Finally, just before serving, poach the eggs. Everyone has their own version of poaching eggs – this is mine. Fill a medium pan with water and bring to a gentle simmer. With a spoon, swirl the water to create a small whirlpool, then crack one of the eggs into the centre. Cook for roughly 2 minutes, remove from the water and drain on kitchen paper. (This step can be done a little in advance, simply dip the eggs in hot water to heat up when needed.)

6 To serve, place a rosti on a small, warm plate. Top with a poached egg and pour over a little warm hollandaise. Garnish with black pepper and chives.

PARSNIP

AND SYRUP CAKE

The parsnip has a sweet, earthy flavour not dissimilar to a carrot (they are closely related), and offers both sweetness and moisture to baking. It can be difficult to detect the parsnip once cooked, which I've seen first hand with unwitting guests who have even complimented the 'normal' cake before any unusual ingredients are divulged.

SERVES 8–10 – PREP TIME: 30 MINUTES
COOK TIME: 55 MINUTES

225g sunflower oil
150g dark brown sugar
3 medium free-range eggs, lightly beaten
60g golden syrup
3 parsnips, peeled and grated (225g peeled weight)
250g self-raising flour
1 teaspoon cinnamon

For the icing
50g unsalted butter, softened
100g cream cheese
150g sifted icing sugar

60g whole pecans, to decorate
900g/2lb loaf tin (23 × 13 × 7cm)

1 Preheat the oven to 180°C/160°C fan/gas mark 4. Grease and line the loaf tin with parchment paper.

2 Take a large bowl and pour in the oil, sugar, eggs and golden syrup. Beat gently using a wooden spoon before adding the grated parsnip.

3 Stir the flour and cinnamon into the mixture and beat to combine – avoid overmixing as this might make the cake a little heavy. Dollop the mixture into the prepared loaf tin and give it a slight shake to create an even level.

4 Bake in the oven for 50–55 minutes until the top of the cake is firm and springs back slightly when pressed. Remove and allow to cool slightly before transferring to a wire rack.

5 To make the icing, beat the softened butter and cream cheese together in a medium bowl with a wooden spoon or electric beaters. The mixture needs to be really smooth as any lumps will be seen when the cake is iced. Slowly stir through the sifted icing sugar. Spread the icing onto your cooled cake and decorate with the whole pecans.

CELERIAC

AND GINGER CUPCAKES WITH LEMON BUTTERCREAM

Some ingredients are takers, seeping up flavour but adding necessary texture and body to dishes. Others are givers, providing punch and flavour, even in small amounts. Celeriac and ginger fall into the latter category. Celeriac is the strong, constant background in this cake while the ginger zings. This recipe has been made for me by the lovely girls at House of Cuckoo who have a disconcerting knack for matching flavours and making vegetable cakes sexy.

MAKES 16 CUPCAKES – PREP TIME: 20 MINUTES
COOK TIME: 25 MINUTES

200g plain flour
½ teaspoon baking powder
½ teaspoon bicarbonate of soda
½ teaspoon salt
2 teaspoons ground ginger
3 medium free-range eggs, room temperature
200g caster sugar
200ml vegetable or rapeseed oil
2 teaspoons good-quality vanilla extract
250g grated fresh celeriac

For the lemon buttercream
80g unsalted butter, at room temperature
250g sifted icing sugar
1 teaspoon vanilla extract
zest of 1 unwaxed lemon
¼ teaspoon fine salt
2 tablespoons milk, or enough for the frosting to reach a piping consistency
fresh unwaxed lemon zest, to decorate

1 Preheat the oven to 180°C/160°C fan/gas mark 4. Line two muffin tins with paper cases. Add the flour, baking powder, bicarbonate of soda, salt and ginger into a large bowl and set aside.

2 Using a mixer, beat the eggs, sugar, oil and vanilla on medium speed until fully combined. Reduce to low speed and add in the grated celeriac. Now slowly add the flour mixture until well combined.

3 Fill each muffin case about two thirds full. The batter will appear quite thin, but don't worry! Bake for about 20–25 minutes, or until a skewer inserted into the middle of a muffin comes out clean. Place on a wire rack to cool for 10 minutes, then take each cupcake out and cool completely before icing.

4 To make the icing, put the butter in a food-processor and beat until light and fluffy, then slowly add the icing sugar. Once combined, and with the food-processor on low, add the vanilla, lemon zest, salt and milk. The consistency should be creamy but still thick. Beat the mixture on medium high for a further 2–3 minutes. The icing should become very light and fluffy.

5 Pipe the buttercream onto your cooled muffins and top with lemon zest.

tip! *Bake flat-topped muffins immediately in the preheated oven. For dome-topped muffins, allow the batter-filled muffin tins to sit for 10–20 minutes before baking.*

CELERIAC

REMOULADE ON PARSNIP SODA BREAD

Celeriac and parsnip aren't the most beautiful of root vegetables, but what they lack in looks they make up for in flavour. Cousins in the root world, their earthy, clean flavours complement each other. This recipe is simple, freshly grated celeriac paired with sharp mayonnaise and bundled onto piping-hot soda bread.

SERVES 4 – COOKING TIME: 45 MINUTES
PREP TIME: 40 MINUTES

1 small celeriac, peeled and thinly sliced
1 tablespoon chopped fresh dill fronds
1 garlic clove
salt and freshly ground black pepper
lemon wedges, to serve

For the mayonnaise
2 free-range egg yolks
2 tablespoons lemon juice
200ml light olive oil
1 tablespoon wholegrain mustard

For the parsnip soda bread
500g wholemeal flour, plus extra for dusting
2 teaspoons bicarbonate of soda
1 teaspoon sea salt
175g parsnips, peeled and grated
100g mature Cheddar cheese, grated
400ml buttermilk
milk (optional)
butter, to serve

1 To make the soda bread, preheat the oven to 200°C/180°C fan/gas mark 6. Sift the flour and bicarbonate of soda into a large mixing bowl and stir in the salt, parsnip and Cheddar.

2 Make a well in the centre of the flour mixture and pour in the buttermilk, stirring as you go. If necessary, add a tablespoon or two of milk to bring the mixture together; it should form a soft dough, just this side of sticky. Shape the dough into a round and using a floured handle of a wooden spoon create a cross on the surface. Place on a baking sheet and bake for 45 minutes.

3 To make the mayonnaise, beat the egg yolks and lemon juice together with a wooden spoon in a medium bowl. Slowly add the oil, constantly beating as you do so. The mixture will become thick and creamy. Stir through the mustard and season well.

4 Drop the celeriac into the mayonnaise and mix well. Add the chopped dill and season well.

5 Slice the soda bread while still warm, rub with a raw clove of garlic and butter generously. Heap on the celeriac remoulade and serve with a wedge of lemon. This isn't a recipe that likes to sit around, so eat immediately before the remoulade has a chance to get 'claggy'.

tip! *Mayonnaise is notoriously difficult to make. If yours begins to split, try adding a drop or two of hot water. If this fails, start again with a new yolk. Slowly pour the 'split' mixture into the new one. This will give you a second chance at mayonnaise success!*

SHEPHERDESS

PIE WITH GARLIC MASH

This lovely, big, family-friendly recipe is ideal for all ages. If you want to be organised, then you can make it in advance and freeze it, then it is a breeze to heat up on the day. All you need is a hot oven and a room full of hungry friends (pictured pages 32–33).

SERVES 8–10 – PREP TIME: 30 MINUTES
COOK TIME: 1 HOUR 40 MINUTES

2 small parsnips, scrubbed clean
200g swede (about ¼ of a swede), peeled and
    cut into 1cm pieces
3 medium carrots, cut into 1cm pieces
300g celeriac (about ½ a celeriac), peeled and
    cubed into 1cm bites
1–2 tablespoons olive oil
1 teaspoon finely chopped rosemary
1 teaspoon mace
salt and freshly ground black pepper

For the sauce
1 onion, sliced
1 teaspoon olive oil

1 teaspoon dried oregano
1 teaspoon dried thyme
250ml red wine
1 tablespoon balsamic vinegar
2 × 400g cans green lentils, drained
500ml good-quality passata

For the garlic mash
1.5kg potatoes, peeled and thickly sliced
3 large garlic cloves
3 tablespoons full-fat crème fraîche
3 tablespoons finely grated Red Leicester cheese

2-litre baking dish

1 Preheat the oven to 200°C/180°C fan/gas mark 6.

2 Peel the parsnip into ribbons using a vegetable peeler and add that to the swede, carrots and celeriac (the ribbons give a nice contrast in size and shape to the other vegetables). Tip the vegetables onto two baking trays and drizzle with 1–2 tablespoons of olive oil. Sprinkle over the rosemary and mace and roast in the hot oven for 25 minutes, ruffling them up halfway through.

3 Meanwhile, to make the sauce, fry the sliced onion in a little oil for a minute or two. Sprinkle over the oregano and thyme and continue to fry until the edges begin to crisp up. Pour over the red wine and allow the mixture to gently bubble until it reduces by half.

4 Add the vinegar, lentils and passata to the pan. Give everything a good stir and cover. Simmer for 25 minutes, stirring every so often. Remove from the heat and empty your roasted root vegetables into the gorgeous tomato lentil sauce. Season well.

5 Meanwhile, half fill a large pan with cold water. Add the potatoes and garlic cloves and bring to the boil. Reduce the heat and simmer for 15–20 minutes until the potatoes cut like butter. Drain and mash well with the crème fraîche.

6 Empty the lentil filling into a 2-litre dish and top with the mash. Sprinkle over the cheese and bake for a further 30–35 minutes at 180°C/160°C fan/gas mark 4.

CARROT

CHICKPEA AND SMOKED PAPRIKA BURGERS

The key to this burger is gram flour, a staple Indian flour made from ground chickpeas, that binds the ingredients together. Allow the mixture to sit for a few minutes before frying, to help the patties 'come together'.

MAKES 10 BURGERS – PREP TIME: 30 MINUTES
COOK TIME: 25 MINUTES

1 tablespoon olive oil
1 red onion, roughly chopped
2 garlic cloves, sliced
1 teaspoon ground cumin
1 teaspoon smoked paprika
1 × 400g can chickpeas, drained
60g dried apricots, chopped
1 teaspoon salt

1 medium free-range egg
3 tablespoons finely chopped coriander
5 tablespoons gram flour
2 carrots, grated
vegetable oil, for brushing
fresh tomato salsa, to serve (see tip below)
handful of rocket leaves, to serve

1 Heat the olive oil in a heavy-based frying pan over a medium heat. Add the red onion and fry for a couple of minutes before adding the garlic and spices. Continue to cook for another minute until the onion is tainted with toasted spices.

2 Place the spiced onion mixture, chickpeas, apricots, salt and egg in a food-processor and blend until you have a paste. Transfer to a bowl before adding the chopped coriander, gram flour and grated carrot. Allow the mixture to sit for 5 minutes – the flour will begin to soak up some of the juices and make the mixture a little more sturdy. Using damp hands, shape the mixture into 10 burgers.

3 Brush each burger with a little oil and place in a hot frying pan or on the BBQ (you may need to work in batches). Cook on each side for 4–5 minutes without moving. Turn the heat down (or move the burgers to a cooler part of the BBQ) until they warm all the way through.

4 Serve topped with tomato salsa and rocket leaves.

tip! *Make a quick salsa with fiercely ripe, finely chopped tomatoes, the juice of a lime, a little finely chopped red onion and some chopped fresh parsley. Serve alongside your burgers.*

CARROT

AND GINGER SOUP WITH SALTED PUMPKIN SEEDS

Bright carrots, spice, fiery ginger and cool crème fraîche – this soup is the perfect tonic for a chilly, rainy day.

MAKES 4 LARGE BOWLS – PREP TIME: 20 MINUTES
COOK TIME: 50 MINUTES

2 tablespoons olive oil
1 onion, roughly chopped
4 garlic cloves, roughly chopped
½ teaspoon turmeric
1 teaspoon ground cumin
pinch of cayenne pepper
1cm piece of fresh ginger, peeled and smashed
700g carrots, sliced into 2.5cm thick rounds
1 large white potato, peeled and cubed

1 litre vegetable stock
salt and freshly ground black pepper

For the topping
oil, for frying
2 tablespoons pumpkin seeds
½ teaspoon salt
4 tablespoons crème fraîche
2 tablespoons chopped coriander

1 Heat the olive oil in a large, heavy-based saucepan and fry the onion until soft, for about 3–4 minutes. Stir through the garlic, turmeric, cumin, cayenne and ginger and continue to cook for 3–4 minutes until the spices smell gorgeous and the garlic has softened.

2 Stir through the carrots and potato. Reduce the heat to low and cook the vegetables, covered, for 20 minutes. Remove the lid and stir occasionally to prevent the soup catching on the base of the pan. Pour over the stock and continue to simmer, uncovered, for a further 20 minutes.

3 Blend the soup in batches until smooth. Season well and set aside.

4 For the topping, heat a little oil in a frying pan until hot. Add the pumpkin seeds and fry until toasted, tossing the pan at regular intervals. Sprinkle the seeds with salt. To serve, top the soup with the salted pumpkin seeds, a dollop of crème fraiche and a little chopped coriander.

HOT-ROASTED

CARROTS

WITH WALNUTS, PARSLEY AND POMEGRANATE

I think you can rarely make too much salad; it can always be used up the following day. This is a simple dish to put together, but the devil is in the detail. Buy young carrots, they will taste better, and do take the time to toast your walnuts; it will only add a layer of flavour.

SERVES 4 – PREP TIME: 15 MINUTES
COOK TIME: 25 MINUTES

600g young carrots, scrubbed and chopped into 2–5cm lengths
1 tablespoon olive oil
1 teaspoon sumac
100g walnuts, chopped
1 small bunch of flat-leaf parsley, chopped
1 pomegranate, deseeded

For the dressing
2 teaspoons runny honey
zest of 1 unwaxed lemon
2 tablespoons red wine vinegar

1 Preheat the oven to 200°C/180°C fan/gas mark 6. Put the carrots in a large roasting tin in an even layer. Drizzle over the olive oil, sprinkle over the sumac and give everything a really good muddle. Roast for 20 minutes or until the carrots are just beginning to caramelise. Add the walnuts to the roasting tin and cook for a further 5 minutes.

2 Meanwhile, make the dressing by putting the honey into a jam jar along with the lemon zest and red wine vinegar. Screw on the lid and shake the jar thoroughly for a few seconds.

3 Remove the hot walnuts and carrots from the oven and mix with the chopped parsley and pomegranate seeds. Pour over the dressing and mix well before spooning into a serving bowl.

CHRISTMAS
CARROT
CAKE

———

If you, like me, tend to miss Stir-up Sunday but feel a sense of duty to provide Christmas cake for the upcoming festivities, there is a solution. Take one solid carrot cake recipe, stir in a whole load of fruit and put it in the oven to bake. The quantities should be roughly 1:1 cake and fruit. Cook until just firm, cover with marzipan and ready-made white icing from packets. Decorate. I can vouch for the fact that this can be done in an afternoon with a one-year-old helping.

MAKES AN 8CM DEEP, 20CM ROUND CAKE – PREP TIME: 45 MINUTES
COOK TIME: 1 HOUR 15 MINUTES

225g unsalted butter, softened
225g light brown sugar
4 medium free-range eggs, beaten
200g carrot, coarsely grated
450g dried mixed fruit
225g self-raising flour
1 teaspoon baking powder
1 teaspoon cinnamon
1 teaspoon mixed spice
pinch of salt

For the icing
2 tablespoons apricot glaze, warmed
icing sugar, to dust
450g golden marzipan
450g white ready-to-roll icing
edible paint, to decorate

20 × 8cm deep spring-form cake tin

1 Preheat the oven to 170°C/150°C fan/gas mark 3½. Line the cake tin with parchment paper.

2 Cream together the butter and sugar in a bowl until pale and fluffy. Beat in the eggs one at a time, mixing well after each addition. Stir through the grated carrot and dried fruit, mixing until everything is evenly distributed.

3 Sift the flour, baking powder, cinnamon, mixed spice and salt into a bowl and add half to the cake mixture. Mix until combined and then add the second half.

4 Spoon the cake mixture into the tin. Bake for between 1 hour 10 minutes and 1 hour 15 minutes, until the cake is springy to the touch and a skewer inserted into the centre comes out clean. Allow the cake to cool in the tin for 10 minutes, then turn out and cool on a wire rack.

5 To marzipan the cake, place the cake on a board. Mix the warmed glaze with a tablespoon of hot water and brush this over the cake. On a surface dusted with icing sugar, roll out the marzipan to a circle just larger than the cake. Lift the marzipan over the cake and ease it to fit smoothly around the sides. Trim off any excess. Lightly brush the marzipan with water.

6 On a surface dusted with icing sugar, roll out the white icing to a large circle. Lift the icing over the cake and ease it to fit smoothly around the sides. Trim off any excess. Dust your palms with icing sugar and gently 'polish' the surface of the icing with the heel of your hand to smooth out any creases. Paint the top of the cake, as you wish, with edible paint.

tip! *If iced, this cake will keep for 3–4 weeks.*

BEETROOT
CHIVE AND CAMEMBERT STRATA

*A strata is a savoury bread pudding, not dissimilar to
a quiche or a bread (pictured pages 40–1).*

SERVES 6 – PREP TIME: 20 MINUTES
COOK TIME: 20 MINUTES

softened butter, for
  greasing
1–2 small raw beetroot
  (about 125g)
5 medium free-range
  eggs
400ml semi-skimmed
  milk
3 tablespoons finely
  chopped chives, plus
  extra for the topping

150g white bread, crusts
  removed, and cut into
  1.5–2cm cubes
125g Camembert
  cheese, cut into thin
  slices
salt and freshly ground
  black pepper

6 × 200ml ramekins or
  a 2-litre ovenproof
  dish

1 Preheat the oven to 180°C/160°C fan/gas mark 4 and
grease the inside of your ramekins with a little soft butter –
you can do this with a buttered finger.

2 Now prepare the beetroot – this is a messy job so you
can use rubber gloves to prevent any hand staining. Use a
grater to coarsely grate the beetroot. Set aside.

3 Beat the eggs, milk and chives together with a fork in
a medium bowl until the eggs have broken up. Season well.
Empty the cubed bread into the bowl and mix to combine.
Allow the mixture to sit for 2–3 minutes.

4 Using a large spoon, spoon enough of the bread
mixture into the ramekins to half fill each one. Divide
the grated beetroot and Camembert slices on top of the
bread and top with further spoonfuls of the bread and egg
mixture until it has all been used up. Finish with a few
more chives and a good grinding of black pepper.

5 Bake for 20 minutes, remove from the oven and eat
immediately while they are still a little puffed up.

BAKED
BEETROOT
QUINOA WITH PINE NUTS

*My aim with this recipe was to create a satisfying vegetarian
dish as a main course without any cheese. I believe I've
succeeded – this is an interesting combination of ingredients,
which uses protein-rich quinoa rather than potatoes.*

SERVES 6 – PREP TIME: 20 MINUTES
COOK TIME: 50 MINUTES

750g raw beetroot
  (about 4)
2 tablespoons olive oil
8 garlic cloves, sliced
a bunch of spring
  onions (5–6), sliced
  diagonally
2 teaspoons dried
  oregano
200g quinoa

1 litre hot vegetable
  stock
50g pine nuts
salt and freshly ground
  black pepper
fresh rocket leaves,
  to serve
thick Greek yogurt,
  to serve

2-litre ovenproof dish

1 Preheat the oven to 200°C/180°C fan/gas mark 6.
Now prepare the beetroot – this is a messy job so you can
use rubber gloves to prevent any hand staining. Peel and
cut each beetroot into thin wedges and put into a roasting
tin. Season well, drizzle over the oil and roast in the hot
oven for 10 minutes before adding the garlic, spring onions
and oregano.

2 Meanwhile, tip the quinoa into a medium saucepan.
Pour over the hot stock and simmer over a medium heat
for 12 minutes. The quinoa is not fully cooked at this stage
and there will be some stock that hasn't been absorbed.

3 Transfer the semi-roasted beetroot into the ovenproof
dish. Add the quinoa, scatter the pine nuts over the surface
and place the dish in the centre of the oven on a baking
tray (this makes it easier to remove from the oven when
hot). Bake for 25–30 minutes. Serve with fresh rocket
leaves and a good dollop of Greek yogurt.

BEETROOT

PARSLEY AND SOURED CREAM TARTS

Brighton is full of delightful independent cafés. Five minutes away from our front door and I'm overwhelmed with coffee jitters, at a loss as to where to place my cappuccino order. My current favourite, nestled in Brighton's North Laines, is aptly named 'Nest' and they serve bold, bright beetroot filo tarts. I love them and so came up with my own version — so now I don't even need to leave the house!

MAKES 8 MINI MUFFIN-SIZE TARTS – PREP TIME: 30 MINUTES
COOK TIME: 20 MINUTES

250g raw beetroot, peeled and cut into
    2.5cm chunks
2 large free-range eggs, beaten
50ml soured cream
100g soft goat's cheese, crumbled

2 tablespoons roughly chopped flat-leaf parsley,
    plus extra to garnish
4 sheets filo pastry
30g butter, melted
salt and freshly ground black pepper

1 Preheat the oven to 190°C/170°C fan/gas mark 5. Make sure you have a non-stick muffin tin.

2 To make the filling, whizz the beetroot chunks in a food-processor until the beetroot is the size of rice grains.

3 Transfer the gloriously coloured mixture to a bowl, stir through the beaten eggs, soured cream, half the goat's cheese and the chopped parsley. Season well.

4 To make the little pastry cases, cut the filo sheets into 10 × 10cm squares. You will need 32 squares in total, 4 squares for each tart.

5 Lay one filo square on your work surface and brush with butter. Lay over a second sheet of filo at a slight angle so that it doesn't cover the first completely and you start to see a star shape appearing. Butter this sheet, then lay over the third sheet, butter it and finally add the fourth filo square. Pick up your 4-sheet filo star with a knife and push it into the centre of a muffin tin. Repeat with all the filo squares to make 8 filo cases.

6 Now spoon the filling equally between the cases and top with the remaining crumbled goat's cheese. Bake for 18–20 minutes until the filling is set and the pastry case is brown. Remove from the oven and sprinkle with fresh parsley. Serve hot, warm or cold, as you like.

tip! *Freeze any leftover filo pastry, well wrapped, until you might need it. You can make an easy canapé with filo pastry — just brush it with butter, roll up into a cigarette shape and sprinkle over Parmesan cheese. Bake at 180°C until golden.*

BEETROOT

ESPRESSO BROWNIES

Such is the brownie's intensity that it can cope seamlessly with an unorthodox intruder. Both the beetroot and the coffee make this particular version sing; it is bitter, but not too much, rich, but not to its detriment, and provides a bit of a 'pick-you-up', courtesy of the coffee!

MAKES 16 BROWNIES – PREP TIME: 25 MINUTES
COOK TIME: 30–35 MINUTES

200g raw beetroot (around 2)
250g dark chocolate (70% cocoa solids)
200g unsalted butter
2 heaped teaspoons instant coffee granules
400g caster sugar

4 medium free-range eggs, beaten
50g cocoa powder
50g plain flour
pinch of salt

20cm square tin with 4cm sides

1 Preheat the oven to 180°C/160°C fan/gas mark 4. Line the tin with parchment paper.

2 Now prepare the beetroot – this is a messy job so you can use rubber gloves to prevent any hand staining. Peel and grate the beetroot on the fine side of a box grater.

3 Melt the chocolate, butter and coffee granules very gently in a large, heavy-based saucepan over a low heat. Remove from the heat and stir in the beetroot, caster sugar and beaten eggs. Combine thoroughly before adding the cocoa powder, plain flour and a pinch of salt. Stir well.

4 Pour the mixture into the prepared tin and bake for 30–35 minutes until just cooked – remember that brownies are easy to overbake. The top should be dried to a paler brown and the middle should still be dark, dense and gooey and only just firm. Allow to cool completely in the tin before slicing, as it will continue to cook until cooled. Serve with strong coffee.

ALLIUM AFICIONADO

Onions, garlic and leeks aren't the most alluring of vegetables but they certainly warrant their very own chapter. I see them as the bridesmaids of the vegetable world, rarely given the importance of a bride's status and often dressed dourly, but do give them time, status and a little imagination and they will fly.

GARLIC

BUTTER ACCORDION LOAF

You cannot make bread without sharing in mind and this loaf is perfect for doing just that. A little tip – don't worry if the bread looks a little messy going into the tin, it will all sort itself out in the oven.

MAKES 1 LOAF PREP – TIME: 30 MINUTES PLUS 2 HOURS PROVING
COOK TIME: 30 MINUTES

1 teaspoon caster sugar
7g fast-action dried yeast
400g white bread flour
1 teaspoon salt
beaten egg, for brushing

For the garlic butter
75g butter, softened
3 tablespoons chopped flat-leaf parsley
10 garlic cloves, crushed
30g Parmesan cheese, finely grated

900g/2lb loaf tin (22 × 11 × 6.5cm)

1 Put the caster sugar, yeast and 250ml lukewarm water into a small bowl and leave for 5 minutes or so until tiny bubbles begin to appear on the surface.

2 Mix together the flour and salt into a large bowl and make a well in the centre. Pour in the yeast mixture and mix well to combine. Turn out the dough onto a well-floured surface and knead for 10 minutes until the dough is smooth and elastic.

3 Cover the dough in oiled clingfilm and leave it to prove in a warm place for 1–2 hours, until the dough has doubled in size.

4 Meanwhile, make the garlic butter by mixing the softened butter, parsley, garlic and half the Parmesan in a small bowl. Set aside.

5 Once the dough has proved, tip it out onto the work surface and knock it back for a minute or so. Roll the dough into an enormous long rectangle, roughly

50 × 20cm. It might take a few minutes to roll it to this size. Spread the rectangle with the garlic butter and fold the rectangle in half lengthways, enclosing the butter.

6 Cut the dough into 8 skinny tiles (scissors are a brilliant tool for this) and place the tiles back to back down the centre of the tin. Don't worry if they look quite small – they grow during the second prove and once they are cooked.

7 Cover the tiles with a tea-towel and leave for a second proving, for 45 minutes to 1 hour.

8 Preheat the oven to 200°C/180°C fan/gas mark 6. Brush your accordion with beaten egg and sprinkle over the remaining Parmesan. Bake for 15 minutes. Turn the heat down to 180°C/160°C fan/gas mark 4 and bake for a further 15 minutes. Remove from the tin and allow to cool for a few minutes before serving.

49

GARLIC
AND WHITE BEAN STEW WITH GREMOLATA

Inspired by the Spanish Caldo Gallego stew, this is a beautiful recipe with simple ingredients. Garlic is the star of the show, but don't be alarmed; the cloves soften in lengthy cooking and provide a gentle backdrop to the white beans. I suggest to serve with a fresh gremolata, but try natural yogurt or pesto, if you prefer.

SERVES 4 – PREP TIME: 15 MINUTES
COOK TIME: 40 MINUTES

20 garlic cloves (about 2 bulbs)
25g salted butter
2 celery sticks, finely sliced into crescents
2 thyme sprigs
200ml white wine
1 × 400g can cannellini beans, drained
1 × 400g can butter beans, drained
2 bay leaves

250ml vegetable stock
75g young leaf spinach
3 tablespoons crème fraîche

For the gremolata
2 tablespoons roughly chopped flat-leaf parsley
1 fat garlic clove, crushed
zest and juice of 2 unwaxed lemons

1 Put the garlic cloves in a medium bowl with their papery jackets still on. Pour over boiling hot water, about 300ml, and leave for 2 minutes. Remove the garlic from the water, keeping the water for later and, as soon as the garlic is cool enough, remove the skins and cut each clove in half lengthways.

2 Melt the butter in a heavy-based saucepan over a low heat. Add the garlic cloves, celery and thyme and cook slowly for 3–4 minutes, being careful not to colour the mix. Pour over the wine and increase the heat, allowing it to bubble and reduce by half.

3 Stir the beans, bay leaves, vegetable stock and garlic water into your pan. Reduce the heat to low and allow the pot to bubble at a languorous pace for 30 minutes, until the sauce has both thickened and reduced in quantity. Use

a potato masher to gently mash some of the mixture at this stage, making the sauce a little thicker. Stir through the young leaf spinach just before serving and allow the leaves to wilt in the warmth of the stew.

4 Meanwhile, make the gremolata by combining the parsley, crushed garlic and lemon zest and juice.

5 Once the beans are beautifully tender remove the pan from the heat. Stir through the crème fraîche and season well. Serve in bowls with a spoonful of gremolata over the top.

SPRING ONION

BLACK RICE AND MANGO SALAD

Black rice, also known in China as `forbidden rice´, was thought to be so nutritionally beneficial that it was only cooked for emperors, such were the high levels of antioxidant and iron. Now the rice is easier to find, although it still seems regal in appearance and texture. Here it sits alongside golden mango, plenty of herbs and an intense soy dressing – an opulent salad of beauty.

SERVES 3–4 – PREP TIME: 20 MINUTES
COOK TIME: 40 MINUTES

150g black rice
6 spring onions, finely sliced
1 large mango, peeled and flesh chopped
   into 1–2cm cubes
4 tablespoons roughly chopped fresh coriander
4 tablespoons roughly chopped fresh mint
zest of 1 large unwaxed lime

For the dressing
2 tablespoons dark soy sauce
juice of 1 lime
5cm piece of ginger, peeled and finely
   grated, juices and all
pinch of salt
pinch of sugar

1 Tip the rice into a small sieve and wash under running water until the water runs clear. Put the rice in a small saucepan and add 450ml cold water. Bring to the boil and simmer for longer than you might expect, for about 35 minutes, until the rice is tender. Drain under cold running water.

2 Make the dressing by combining all the ingredients in a bowl. Taste and adjust the seasoning to taste, adding in a little more sugar, salt or lime zest, as you like.

3 In a big bowl mix the black rice, spring onions (reserving a few for garnish), the mango chunks, chopped herbs, lime zest and dressing. Serve, dressed with a few bright green spring onions.

ROASTED
SHALLOT
ROSEMARY AND RICOTTA TART

Banana shallots or echalions are the torpedo-shaped shallot, rather than the smaller, rounder version. Larger, at 8–10cm long, and easier to peel, they are certainly better to deal with and have a delicate flavour, perfect for the centrepiece of this simple tart.

SERVES 8 – PREP TIME: 1 HOUR
COOK TIME: 1 HOUR 15 MINUTES

For the pastry
200g plain flour
generous pinch of salt
100g cold salted butter, cut into small cubes
30g Parmesan cheese
1 medium free-range egg yolk, beaten

For the tart
600g banana shallots, cut into quarters lengthways
1 tablespoon olive oil

a few sprigs of rosemary, leaves stripped and
     finely chopped
2 teaspoons light brown sugar
250g ricotta
3 free-range medium eggs, lightly whisked
50g crème fraîche
50g Gruyère cheese, finely grated
salt and cracked black pepper

21cm square or 23cm round tart tin

1 To make the pastry, sift the flour and salt into a large mixing bowl. Add the cubed butter and, using your fingertips and thumbs, gently rub the butter into the flour until it resembles breadcrumbs. Add the Parmesan and rub again until the cheese is evenly mixed through.

2 Add the beaten egg yolk and 2 tablespoons cold water and use a palette knife or a round-bladed knife to bring the dough together, adding another tablespoon of water if it is too dry. Gather the dough up in your hands and knead very briefly before wrapping it in clingfilm and putting it straight in the fridge until needed.

3 To make the tart, preheat the oven to 200°C/180°C fan/gas mark 6. On a lightly floured surface, roll out the pastry to about 3mm thick and line your tart tin as neatly as possible. Trim the edges, then prick the base with a fork and return it to the fridge for 20 minutes – this prevents shrinkage when it goes in the oven.

4 Toss the shallots in olive oil with half the rosemary. Sprinkle over the brown sugar and roast in the preheated oven for 25 minutes, moving the shallots around half way through the cooking time. Remove the shallots and reduce the oven temperature to 180°C/160°C fan/gas mark 4.

5 Remove the pastry case from the fridge, line with baking parchment and fill with baking beans. Blind bake for 25 minutes, removing the paper and beans for the final 5 minutes of cooking time.

6 In a large bowl, beat together the ricotta, eggs, crème fraîche and Gruyère. Add two-thirds of the roasted onions, keeping some back for the top of the tart. Stir the ingredients well so the shallots are coated, season and put the mixture in the pre-baked tart case. Top with the reserved shallots, the remaining rosemary and plenty of cracked black pepper. Cook for 25 minutes until the filling has puffed up and is firm to the touch.

CHARRED
ONIONS
ON AVOCADO AND RYE

Some friends and I visited Copenhagen for a weekend and ate the most superior rye bread I'd ever tasted. The backbone of many a school lunchbox and smørrebrød, Danish rye bread is made with the rye grain. The bread is rich and heavier than you might expect so perfect to hold an open sandwich. Creamy avocado and slowly fried onion make a slice of rye fit for lunch.

SERVES 2 – PREP TIME: 10 MINUTES
COOK TIME: 5 MINUTES

1 tablespoon olive oil
1 red onion, sliced
1 ripe avocado, roughly chopped
juice of ½ lime
½ red chilli, deseeded and finely chopped

½ tablespoon roughly chopped coriander,
   plus a few leaves to garnish
¼ teaspoon sea salt
freshly ground black pepper
3 small slices of rye bread
1 garlic clove, sliced in half

1 Heat the oil in a large frying pan until hot and throw in the onion. Cook for 6–7 minutes over a medium heat, stirring regularly, until it's just beginning to crisp and char. Don't stop cooking too early; a little crunch will add lovely texture.

2 While the onions are cooking, place the avocado in a bowl with the lime juice, chilli and chopped coriander. Gently smash with a fork and season with salt and pepper.

3 Toast or grill the rye bread slices when you are ready to serve. Rub the halved garlic clove over the slices and top with the avocado smash. Spoon over your crunchy onion, followed by a leaf or two of fresh coriander. Serve immediately.

ONION

WITH LEBANESE LENTILS AND RICE

This is a surprising recipe – think Middle Eastern comfort food stacked full of nutrients and flavour. Perfectly cooked lentils are tossed with rice, caramelised onions and spice and spiked with bold, fresh mint and sharp lemon. Serve with thick yogurt and warm flatbread.

SERVES 4 – PREP TIME: 25 MINUTES
COOK TIME: 1 HOUR

200g dried green lentils
1 tablespoon vegetable oil
1 teaspoon cumin seeds
½ teaspoon cracked black pepper
3 onions, sliced
100g basmati rice
1 cinnamon stick
½ teaspoon ground allspice
2 cardamom pods
600ml hot vegetable stock

For the dressing
2 tablespoons chopped mint, plus a little
   extra to garnish
juice of 3 lemons
100ml extra virgin olive oil
3 garlic cloves, chopped

1 Rinse the lentils under running water and tip them into a small saucepan. Cover the lentils generously with cold water and bring the pan to a boil. Reduce the heat and simmer the lentils for about 20 minutes until they are cooked through but not mushy.

2 Meanwhile heat the vegetable oil in a heavy-based saucepan on a low heat. Add the cumin seeds and pepper and fry for a minute or two before adding the sliced onions. Cook for around 15–20 minutes until brown and starting to char on the edges. Remove a third of the onion and set aside for the garnish.

3 Stir the rice, cinnamon stick, allspice and cardamom pods into the onions. Cook for a minute or two before adding the stock. Cook the rice for 5 minutes before adding the cooked lentils. Cover and simmer on a medium low heat for 20 minutes. By this time the liquid should be totally absorbed. Turn off the heat and allow the pot to stand for 5 minutes.

4 Meanwhile make the dressing by combining all the ingredients in a jug, mixing well until amalgamated and then pour the dressing over the rice and lentil mixture. Pile into a warm bowl and garnish with the remaining onions and some freshly chopped mint.

SWEET ONION

WITH CORN BREAD

For an ubiquitous, humble and unfailingly cheap vegetable, onions are extremely versatile and can be totally transformed so they become the star of the dish. In this recipe, the onions are cooked slowly with a handful of Southern American flavours – cocoa, chilli, black beans and sweetcorn – then topped with fresh cornbread. Serve with soured cream and fresh lime for the ultimate one-pot meal.

SERVES 6 – PREP TIME: 25 MINUTES
COOK TIME: 1 HOUR

2 tablespoons vegetable oil
2 white onions, sliced
2 red onions, sliced
1 green pepper, roughly chopped
2 garlic cloves, thinly sliced
1 teaspoon dried oregano
1 teaspoon ground cumin
1 teaspoon chilli powder
1 tablespoon cocoa powder
2 tablespoons tomato purée
1 × 400g can chopped tomatoes
1 × 400g can black beans, drained
1 × 200g can sweetcorn, drained
salt and freshly ground black pepper

For the cornbread
250ml milk
2 medium free-range eggs, beaten lightly
1 green chilli, finely chopped
50g strong plain flour or bread flour
120g polenta
1 tablespoon caster sugar
2 teaspoons baking powder
1 teaspoon ground coriander

soured cream, to serve
50g Cheddar cheese, grated, to serve

2-litre ovenproof dish

1 Heat the oil in a large saucepan. Add the onions and green pepper and fry over a medium heat until they begin to soften. Continue to cook, gently for about 10 minutes, until they are soft and a little gloopy. Stir through the garlic, oregano, cumin and chilli powder. Turn up the heat slightly and stir through the cocoa powder and tomato purée. Finally add the chopped tomatoes and 150ml water. Season well, cover with a lid and simmer for 15 minutes, stirring every so often.

2 Preheat the oven to 180°C/160°C fan/gas mark 4. To make the cornbread, whisk the milk and eggs in a large bowl and add the chilli. In a separate bowl combine the flour, polenta, sugar, baking powder and coriander and mix well. Combine the dry ingredients with the wet and stir to combine. This mixture will be of quite a liquid consistency at this point but it will thicken in the oven.

3 Add the black beans and sweetcorn to the tomato mixture and stir to combine. If needed, add a little more water so that the consistency is similar to a bolognaise. Put the mixture into a 2-litre dish. Spoon or pour the polenta mixture on the top – be gentle as you want it to sit on top of the mixture rather than be lost inside.

4 Bake for 25 minutes until the polenta topping has set. Serve with soured cream and grated Cheddar.

RED ONION

BULGAR WHEAT WITH HALLOUMI AND GARLIC AND TREACLE PESTO

Mellow roasted garlic blended with bittersweet treacle, toasted pine nuts and Parmesan is pure luxury and can fit into the pesto bracket. Pair this with salty fried halloumi and a fresh bulgar wheat salad and your table will be set for a marvellous supper.

SERVES 4 – PREP TIME: 25 MINUTES – COOK TIME: 35 MINUTES

For the bulgar wheat salad
1 tablespoon olive oil
2 large red onions or 3 small onions, cut
   into wedges
4 garlic cloves, thinly sliced
1 teaspoon cinnamon
550ml hot vegetable stock
175g bulgar wheat
3 tablespoons roughly chopped flat-leaf parsley
250g halloumi cheese, cut into thick slices

For the pesto
3 whole garlic bulbs
100g pine nuts, toasted
1 tablespoon black treacle
good pinch of sea salt
50g Parmesan cheese, very finely grated
80–90ml olive oil

1 First things first, make your pesto. This can be done 2–3 days before you want to eat. The trick is to remember to do this when you are using the oven for something else – it seems wasteful for a hot oven to be used for teeny garlic bulbs. Roast the whole garlic bulbs, peel and all, at 200°C/180°C fan/gas mark 6 for 20 minutes.

2 Remove the bulbs from the oven and leave them for a few minutes until they are cool enough to handle. Using your fingers, squidge out the sweet roasted purée from the inside of the bulbs.

3 Using a food-processor or a hand-held blender, mix the garlic, toasted pine nuts, black treacle, salt and Parmesan. Slowly pour olive oil in the mixture, adding a little more if needed, and mix well to incorporate. Set aside.

4 To make the bulgar wheat salad, heat a large frying pan over a high heat and add the oil. Once hot, tip in your onion wedges and fry for a minute or two before adding the garlic and cinnamon.

5 Meanwhile, pour the vegetable stock into a small pan and bring to a simmer over a medium heat. Add the bulgar wheat and gently cook for 8–10 minutes until the grains are bloated and cooked through. Remove from the heat and stir through the red onion mixture and chopped parsley.

6 Heat the empty frying pan over a high heat and add the halloumi slices. Fry for a minute or two on each side until they begin to char. Remove from the pan and serve on plates with a heap of bulgar wheat and a good dollop of roasted garlic pesto.

LEEK
AND STUFFING HAMPER

This recipe is for those moments when a sense of occasion is needed.

SERVES 6 – PREP TIME: 1 HOUR – COOK TIME: 1 HOUR

4 long, slender leeks (about 650g in weight and
   30cm long), cut in half lengthways
2 tablespoons olive oil
1 tablespoon Dijon mustard
1 tablespoon mature Cheddar cheese, finely grated

For the stuffing
olive oil, for frying
1 large onion, finely chopped
3 garlic cloves, finely chopped
½ teaspoon fennel seeds, crushed
1 teaspoon coriander seeds, crushed

50g dried apricots, roughly chopped
1 large apple, grated
1 tablespoon cider vinegar
50g dried breadcrumbs
150g crème fraîche
salt and freshly ground black pepper

For the pastry
300g plain flour
110g cold butter, cut into roughly 2cm cubes
pinch of salt
beaten egg, to glaze

1 First, make your pastry. Pulse the flour, butter and salt in a blender or food-processor until it resembles breadcrumbs. Add 2 tablespoons of cold water, or enough to just bind your pastry. Bring the pastry together, wrap it in clingfilm and chill for 15 minutes in the fridge.

2 Meanwhile, preheat the oven to 200°C/180°C fan/gas mark 6. To make the filling, place the leeks on a baking sheet. Drizzle over the olive oil and pop them into the oven for 20 minutes. Remove the leeks and allow to cool. Reduce the oven to 180°C/160°C fan/gas mark 4.

3 To make the stuffing, heat a little olive oil in a large frying pan and fry the onion over a medium heat. Add the garlic, fennel and coriander seeds after a minute, and continue to fry the onion until translucent and soft. Tip in the apricots, apple and vinegar and cook for 2–3 minutes. Everything should now be soft and steamy. Season well and add the breadcrumbs, then stir in the crème fraîche. Maintain the heat until all the ingredients have glued together. Season well and set aside to cool for a good 10 minutes.

4 Roll out the chilled pastry to a 30 × 40cm rectangle, removing any excess pastry – you need straight edges! Score two lines down the length of the pastry to roughly divide it into three equal rectangles. Using a sharp knife, slice the pastry horizontally at roughly 1.5cm intervals down the length of either side, leaving the central third untouched. You are creating lengths to help form your plait. Gently transfer the pastry to a baking sheet.

5 Spoon your cool stuffing down the centre and lay the leeks on top. They should be evenly distributed down the length of the pastry. Take the tablespoon of Dijon mustard and spread it on top. Sprinkle over the Cheddar cheese.

6 Now create your plait. Starting at the top, fold one little pastry length over the filling and then take the opposite one and fold it to meet in the middle. Continue down the length of the hamper, tucking the last two under the base of the pastry. Brush beaten egg over the pastry before baking in the hot oven for 30–35 minutes until it has a lovely golden tinge.

LEEKS

WITH TARRAGON CRUMBLE

Here is a quick recipe that gives the crumble, our English national treasure, a savoury slant. Leeks, mustard and white sauce form a moreish base and a herby, cheesy crumble sits on top catching the escaping juices.

SERVES 4 – PREP TIME: 20 MINUTES
COOK TIME: 40 MINUTES

4 leeks, cut into 1–2cm rounds
a thick slice of butter
1 tablespoon plain flour
200ml hot vegetable stock
200ml semi-skimmed milk
1 tablespoon wholegrain mustard
salt and freshly ground black pepper

For the crumble:
150g butter, softened
300g plain flour
2 tablespoons roughly chopped tarragon leaves
1 teaspoon English mustard powder
80g grated Cheddar cheese

1.5-litre ovenproof dish

1 Preheat the oven to 180°C/160°C fan/gas mark 4. Put the leeks in a large pan with the butter. Cover and gently sweat the leeks over a medium low heat for 10–12 minutes, until they have softened and cooked through but not coloured. Stir occasionally to prevent the leeks catching on the bottom of the pan.

2 Add the plain flour to the leeks and stir it through until it has all but disappeared. Pour in the stock, milk and mustard, season and simmer gently for 5 minutes.

3 Empty the creamy leeks into a 1.5-litre ovenproof dish. Set aside to cool a little.

4 To make the crumble, rub the softened butter into the flour until the mixture resembles fine breadcrumbs – your hands are the best tool for this job. Add the tarragon, mustard powder and grated Cheddar cheese. Mix thoroughly, creating small clusters of crumble mix. Use your hands to clump the mixture together a little, adding a few drops of water if needed. Liberally sprinkle the crumble on top of the creamy leek mix and press down gently.

5 Bake in the hot oven for 25 minutes until the crumble is golden brown and the leeks are bubbling up from the bottom.

BEANS
& SUMMER
GREENS

The handsome chapter. The salads, soups and light meals that make you want to book holidays and drop a dress size. This collection also includes radish and sweetcorn: though they are not greens, they reach their peak in summer and hanker for a place on the menu. The colours remind us that there is no substitute for nature. Never could you replicate the elegant green of a chard in fabric or hope to have the vivacious red of a radish reproduced on your dining room walls. We must be content to simply enjoy their vibrancy on our plates.

LETTUCE

SOUP

My evenings are often spent reading Beatrix Potter and pondering Mr McGregor's garden with my little boy. He loves the thought of a rabbit getting lost among the lettuces, not being quite tall enough to see the garden gate. This soup is wonderfully simple and fresh, lovely for a summer lunch just as it is; alternatively, it can be made glamorous with a swirl of cream and some crispy bruschetta.

MAKES 1.5 LITRES – PREP TIME: 25 MINUTES
COOK TIME: 20 MINUTES

1 round lettuce
3 tablespoons salted butter
3 shallots, finely sliced
3 fat garlic cloves, sliced
400g frozen petits pois
1.5 litres hot vegetable stock

small bunch of mint leaves
½ teaspoon salt
½ teaspoon caster sugar
freshly ground black pepper
warm, buttered bread, to serve

1 Separate the lettuce leaves and wash thoroughly to remove any clinging grit. Melt the butter in a large, deep saucepan over a medium heat and add the shallots and garlic. Gently fry for 6–8 minutes, until the shallots are soft, turning the heat down if necessary.

2 When the shallots are tender but not brown, chop the lettuce up a bit and stir it into the butter. When it has wilted, tip in the peas, the stock and the mint leaves and bring to the boil. Turn the heat down, season with salt, sugar and black pepper and simmer for 7–10 minutes.

3 Remove the pan from the heat and blend the soup in a liquidiser. Carefully return to the pan to reheat gently, check the seasoning and serve in big bowls with warm, buttered bread.

ROCKET

RASPBERRY AND GORGONZOLA SALAD

I've eaten something similar to this salad in the beautiful Olympic café in Kalk Bay, which sells some of the best coffee in South Africa. They don't bother with the usual formal café rules, and operate as a hotch-potch of rustic charm and enviable style. Do try to find raspberry vinegar for the dressing – it's a valuable ingredient to have in your store cupboard – but if you find it hard to come by use white wine vinegar instead. If you're a vegetarian, use a vegetarian alternative to gorgonzola, such as dolcelatte.

SERVES 4 – PREP TIME: 20 MINUTES
COOK TIME: 8–10 MINUTES

2 tablespoons olive oil
2 big chunks of brown bread, cut into croûtons
½ teaspoon salt
200g raspberries, the plumpest you can find
70g wild rocket
150g Gorgonzola, pulled into chunks

For the dressing
2 tablespoons raspberry vinegar
1 teaspoon Dijon mustard
2 tablespoons extra virgin olive oil

1 You need to make the croûtons first so they aren't too hot when they hit the salad leaves. Heat the oil in a medium frying pan and when the oil is sparking a little, add the bread. When the croûtons are in the pan, throw over a little salt and fry until they all have a crunch. Keep tossing the pan so one side doesn't colour more than the other.

2 To make the dressing, put all the ingredients in a jug and mix as thoroughly as you can – do this without the dressing jumping out of the jug and staining your shirt!

3 Combine the raspberries, rocket and Gorgonzola in a bowl and pour over the dressing. Toss together (gently so you don't bruise any of those rocket leaves) and add the croûtons. Serve in a big pile on an even bigger plate.

SPINACH

BLUEBERRY AND CUCUMBER COUSCOUS
WITH LEMON HOUMOUS

Splash out on some beautiful plump blueberries – they can make this dish and add a surprisingly bite of sweetness to a tart, savoury salad. Substitute couscous with brown rice, quinoa or barley for an alternative grain salad.

SERVES 2–3 – PREP TIME: 25 MINUTES
COOK TIME: 6 MINUTES

150g couscous
250ml hot vegetable stock
50g young leaf spinach
½ cucumber, cut into rounds
zest of 2 unwaxed lemons
125g soft, crumbly goat's cheese
100g blueberries
1 tablespoon olive oil

For the houmous
1 × 400g can chickpeas, drained and rinsed
4 tablespoons tahini
2 small garlic cloves
juice of 2 lemons
sea salt

1 First make the houmous. Put the chickpeas into a blender or food-processor with the tahini, garlic, lemon juice, salt and 2–3 tablespoons cold water. Whizz to a smooth paste, adding a little water until the houmous reaches the desired consistency. Set aside while you make the salad.

2 Toast the couscous by putting a heavy-based frying pan over a medium–high heat and add the couscous to the dry pan. Toss the couscous around the pan until it starts to turn golden, for about 4–5 minutes. Remove from the heat and add the hot stock. There will be steam and fury. Leave the couscous to soak up the liquid for a few minutes, stirring once or twice to ensure the stock is evenly distributed.

3 Put the couscous into a bowl and add the spinach, cucumber, lemon zest, goat's cheese and blueberries (keeping back a few blueberries, some goat's cheese and lemon zest for garnish). Add the olive oil and combine well.

4 Pile the salad onto a plate and top with the reserved blueberries, goat's cheese and lemon zest. Serve with a bowl of the houmous.

SPINACH
AND LEMON BAGUETTES

Sometimes homemade pastry is one step too far. This recipe is for those moments, when you are motivated enough to make a picnic but have only the energy to buy a baguette. The lemon flavour sings and sits beautifully next to the spinach.

MAKES I BAGUETTE – PREP TIME: 15 MINUTES
COOK TIME: 35 MINUTES

1 baguette
200g young leaf spinach
200ml double cream
2 medium free-range eggs, beaten
1 garlic clove, crushed

zest of 1 large unwaxed lemon
1 teaspoon English mustard
75g Gruyère cheese, finely grated
salt and freshly ground black pepper

1 Preheat the oven to 180°C/160°C fan/gas mark 4. Half the baguette, then hollow out each half by cutting an oval from the top of the bread with a sharp bread knife. Remove the 'lid' and, using your hands, take out the inside of the baguette leaving a healthy amount of crust – you want it to be watertight!

2 Boil a full kettle of water and put the spinach in a large sieve or colander. Pour over the water and allow the spinach to wilt. Set aside to cool.

3 In a medium bowl mix the double cream, eggs, garlic, lemon zest and mustard. Squeeze any excess water from the wilted spinach and put onto a board. Roughly chop and stir into the mixture along with half of the Gruyère. Season well.

4 Spoon the mixture into each baguette half and sprinkle over the remaining cheese. Bake for 30–35 minutes until the filling has just set. Allow it to sit for a few minutes until ready to serve, or wait until it is completely cold.

tip! *You might find that your baguette is slightly skinnier or fatter than the one in the picture; just remove the centre and pour in as much filling as you are able. Any excess can be baked in muffin cases!*

SPINACH

AND BLOOD ORANGE SALAD
WITH WHEAT BERRIES

Here's a salad suitable for winter when colds are rife and vitamin C is needed more than ever. Wheat berries are wonderfully robust and filling – all they require is flavourful ingredients to really set them off. I often serve this with an oily fish such as mackerel.

SERVES 4 – PREP TIME: 25 MINUTES
COOK TIME: 45 MINUTES

275g wheat berries
70g young leaf spinach
2 blood oranges, peeled and sliced
100g feta cheese, crumbled

For the dressing
2 tablespoons extra virgin olive oil
zest and juice of 1 blood orange
2 shallots, very finely chopped
1 tablespoon cider vinegar
2 tablespoons finely chopped fresh dill fronds
2 tablespoons finely chopped flat-leaf parsley

1 Begin by cooking the wheat berries. Place them in a pan and add water until they are covered by about 8cm. Bring to the boil. Reduce the heat and simmer, uncovered, until the wheat berries are tender but still chewy, for about 45 minutes. Drain in a sieve and empty the wheat berries onto a baking sheet to cool in a single layer.

2 Once the wheat berries are cool, toss them with the spinach, blood oranges and feta.

3 Make the dressing by whisking the oil, orange zest and juice, shallot, vinegar and herbs in a small bowl. Pour the dressing over the salad and serve up for a satisfying dinner on a frosty day.

variations

Use this recipe as a starting point: if you aren't able to find wheat berries, substitute pearl barley; and if blood oranges aren't in season, use normal ones – it will be just as delicious.

ARTICHOKE

WITH LEMON AND BUTTER

The globe artichoke is a feat of natural engineering and tastes as complex as its appearance. There aren't too many vegetables that you could place in the centre of the table that will look so completely glamorous, simply dressed in butter and lemon.

SERVES 1 – PREP TIME: 10 MINUTES
COOK TIME: 35 MINUTES

1 artichoke
½ lemon, sliced

50g butter, melted

1 Remove any smaller leaves towards the base of the artichoke, remove the stem so the artichoke can sit on a surface and gently wash it under cold water.

2 Half fill a large pan with lightly salted water and bring to the boil. Add the lemon slices. Put the whole artichoke in the pot and cover. Simmer for 30–35 minutes – the cooking time varies depending on the size of your artichoke, but a good test is being able to easily pull a leaf from the centre.

3 To eat, break off each petal, one at a time, and dip the white fleshy end into the melted butter. Tightly grip the other end of the petal, put it in your mouth, dip-side down, and pull through your teeth to remove a soft, pulpy, delicious portion before discarding the rest. Continue until you have eaten all of the little petals!

4 When you reach the fuzzy part (called the 'choke'), remove it with a knife or spoon, discarding each bit as you scrape them off. The remaining bottom of the artichoke is the heart. Cut this into pieces and dip it into the melted butter. Done.

ARTICHOKE

PUY LENTIL AND PINE NUT SALAD

This recipe can be cooked and assembled in 15 minutes; it really couldn't be simpler. My tip would be to buy good-quality, cooked lentils (often sold in pouches), which are a delicious backbone to any salad. The same applies to the artichokes. Once they have been sourced, preparation is minimal and the result is completely delicious. Eat warm or cold, whatever suits.

SERVES 2 – PREP TIME: 10 MINUTES
COOK TIME: 3–4 MINUTES

40g pine nuts
200g cooked, marinated artichoke hearts, drained
1 small red onion, finely chopped
250g cooked Puy lentils
3 tablespoons chopped flat-leaf parsley

For the dressing
1 tablespoon cider vinegar or white wine vinegar
3 tablespoons extra virgin olive oil
¾ teaspoon Dijon mustard

1 Heat a frying pan over a medium heat and add the pine nuts. Toast for 3–4 minutes until charred. Don't be tempted to leave your post as nut toaster – they will go from charred to burnt as soon as your back is turned.

2 For the dressing, put the vinegar, olive oil and mustard into a jam jar. Screw on the lid and shake vigorously until you have a lovely thick dressing. Season to taste.

3 Chop any large pieces of the artichoke hearts in half. In a medium bowl mix the artichoke hearts, onion, lentils, parsley and three-quarters of the pine nuts. Pour over the dressing and combine all the ingredients thoroughly. Serve, garnished with the remaining pine nuts.

tip! *If you would like to give your artichoke hearts another layer of flavour simply sear them on a hot griddle or fry for 2–3 minutes until the outer leaves begin to char.*

PEA

MOZZARELLA AND LEMON TART

This is a real treat of a tart to come home to. Quite simply, peas, garlic and ricotta are slathered on puff pastry and cooked for a few minutes. Then, to give it a professional finish, all you need is a handful of cress, mint and lemon zest, to garnish.

SERVES 4–6 – PREP TIME: 15 MINUTES, PLUS 10 MINUTES DEFROSTING
COOK TIME: 35 MINUTES

500g block of puff pastry
200g frozen peas, left to defrost for 10–15 minutes
3 garlic cloves
250g ricotta, strained of excess water
1 medium free-range egg

1 × 200g mozzarella ball, torn
salt and freshly ground black pepper
zest of 1 unwaxed lemon, to garnish
3 tablespoons freshly chopped mint, to garnish
cress, to garnish

1 Preheat the oven to 200°C/180°C fan/gas mark 6. Roll the puff pastry into a rectangle of 30 × 25cm. Slide the pastry onto a floured baking sheet and top with a second baking sheet (this acts as a weight while the pastry cooks and prevents it rising too much).

2 Bake the pastry for 20 minutes and remove from the oven. If the base has still puffed up despite the weight, then gently press the top baking sheet down to flatten the pastry. Allow to cool for a minute or two.

3 Tip three-quarters of the peas and garlic cloves and 1–2 tablespoons water into a blender and blitz until you have a lovely rough, bright green paste. In a separate bowl, mix the ricotta and egg. Add the green pea mixture to the fresh ricotta and mix very lightly so there are still visible pockets of green and white.

4 Dollop the combined mixture onto the tart base. Top with the remaining whole peas and torn mozzarella. Season with salt and black pepper and bake for 15 minutes, or until the ricotta has puffed slightly and the edges are beginning to brown.

5 Remove from the oven and garnish with lemon zest, mint and cress. Serve immediately, in generous squares.

PEA

CRÈME FRAÎCHE AND MINT GNOCCHI

I once read a description of gnocchi as bloated pasta, which I think is a gorgeous explanation. They have the texture of a dumpling and provide a similar, comforting element to a meal. This is my favourite fast supper and one that we have on an almost weekly basis.

SERVES 3–4 – PREP TIME: 10 MINUTES
COOK TIME: 30 MINUTES

a little butter, for greasing
800g gnocchi
300g frozen peas
3 garlic cloves, crushed
a bunch of mint, leaves picked and chopped
300g crème fraîche
a good grating of Parmesan cheese
salt and freshly ground black pepper

2-litre ovenproof dish

1 Preheat the oven to 200°C/180°C fan/gas mark 6. Lightly butter the inside of a 2-litre ovenproof dish.

2 Bring a large pan of water to the boil. Working quickly, add the gnocchi and peas. Bring the water back to the boil and simmer for 3 minutes, until the gnocchi is bobbing on the surface of the water. Drain straight away. Return the gnocchi and peas to the saucepan and stir through the crushed garlic and mint. Add the crème fraîche. Mix until all the ingredients are evenly distributed and then season well with black pepper and a little salt.

3 Transfer the contents of the pan to the greased dish, level the surface, scatter with Parmesan and cook, covered, in the preheated oven for 20–25 minutes, until the gnocchi has puffed a little. Serve straight from the oven.

ASPARAGUS

AND MASCARPONE ORECCHIETTE

Often I think the best dishes consist of three or four ingredients, with no one ingredient clamouring for attention, and each one speaking for itself. This is a really quick recipe, ideal for the middle of the week when all you want to do is get home, eat and then sleep.

SERVES 4 – PREP TIME: 15 MINUTES
COOK TIME: 15 MINUTES

a pinch of sea salt
400g dried orecchiette
200g asparagus tips, each cut into 3cm lengths
a large knob of butter
5 garlic cloves, finely chopped
50g hazelnuts with skins, roughly chopped
125g mascarpone
salt and freshly ground black pepper

1 Bring a deep pan of water to the boil and add a generous pinch of salt. Add the pasta and boil for 5 minutes before throwing the asparagus tips into the simmering water. Continue to cook for 5 minutes until the pasta is al dente and the asparagus is just tender. Drain in a colander, reserving a cup or so of the cooking liquid. Return the asparagus and pasta back to the saucepan.

2 Meanwhile melt the butter in a small frying pan and, once bubbling, throw in the garlic and chopped hazelnuts. Cook for a minute or two before stirring this mixture through the asparagus and cooked pasta, making sure the garlic is evenly distributed.

3 Return the pan to a low heat and add dollops of mascarpone. Slowly stir until the mascarpone has melted and the pasta is coated with a lovely creamy sauce. Add a little of the pasta water to loosen the sauce if needed. Season and serve at once.

DANCING
ASPARAGUS
AND GOAT'S CHEESE TART

A playful and fresh tart that celebrates the moment spring has sprung.

SERVES 6 – PREP TIME: 20 MINUTES, PLUS 45 MINUTES CHILLING
COOK TIME: 55 MINUTES

For the pastry
250g plain flour
125g cold butter, cut into 2cm cubes
pinch of salt
pinch of ground paprika

For the tart
250g asparagus spears
1–2 tablespoons Dijon mustard

100g soft, crumbly goat's cheese
1 medium free-range egg plus 1 medium
    free-range egg yolk
125ml double cream
40g finely grated Cheddar cheese
sea salt and freshly ground black pepper

rectangular tin (about 36 × 12 × 3cm)

1 Make the pastry by pulsing the flour, butter, salt and paprika in a blender or food-processor until it resembles breadcrumbs. Add 2 tablespoons cold water, or just enough to bind your pastry. Bring the pastry together, wrap it in clingfilm and chill for 15 minutes in the fridge.

2 To blanch the asparagus, half fill a shallow pan with water. Snap off the bottom of the asparagus spears – as these can be quite tough – and cut the stems into 2.5cm pieces. Drop the sliced spears into the simmering water and blanch for 4 minutes before draining and immediately running under cold water. This prevents further cooking and protects the gorgeous green colour.

3 On a floured surface, roll your pastry to a thickness of around 3mm. Carefully line your rectangular tin, cutting off any excess pastry. Chill the pastry in the fridge for 30 minutes – this helps prevent shrinkage in the oven.

4 Preheat the oven to 190°C/170°C fan/gas mark 5. Line your tart case with baking paper and fill it with baking beans. Place the case on a baking sheet and cook for 20 minutes. Remove the baking beans and the paper and return the cases to the oven for a further 5 minutes. The base of the case should now feel dry to the touch. On removing the tart case from the oven, reduce the temperature to 180°C/160°C fan/gas mark 4.

5 Using the back of a spoon, smother Dijon mustard on the base of your case. Using your fingers, crumble goat's cheese around the outside edge of the pastry creating an empty lake in the middle. Add two-thirds of the blanched spears to the centre in a higgledy-piggledy manner, with some lying flat and some standing upright.

6 Gently beat together the egg, egg yolk and cream and season well. Gently spoon the custard into the tart, making sure it fills each corner. Now lay the remaining spears over your custard so they are not hidden. Add the grated cheese and bake for 30 minutes. Serve hot, warm or cold accompanied with pea shoots, if you fancy.

RAINBOW CHARD

MOZZARELLA AND HERB PANZANELLA

The scarlet stems and red-veined leaves of rainbow chard would surely win any garden beauty pageant and although the colour diminishes a little in cooking, the taste only improves. The general rule with chard is to cook the leaves as you would spinach and the stalks as you would asparagus (pictured on pages 84–85).

SERVES 6 – PREP TIME: 40 MINUTES
COOK TIME: 10 MINUTES

300g rainbow chard
a thick slice of butter
3 garlic cloves, crushed
4–5 slices day-old ciabatta (roughly 100g)
1 × 200g ball of mozzarella
2 heaped tablespoons tarragon leaves
2 tablespoons chopped flat-leaf parsley

1 heaped tablespoon chopped dill fronds
100g pine nuts
salt and freshly ground black pepper

For the dressing
4 tablespoons extra virgin olive oil
juice of 1 lemon

1 Start by cooking the beautiful chard. Remove any tough-looking leaves and roughly chop the stems and leaves into 4cm chunks. Heat the butter in a medium shallow pan over a medium heat. Add the garlic and chard. Stir well and put the lid on. Steam for 3–4 minutes and remove immediately before all colour has left the stems.

2 Tear or cube the bread into 2–3cm chunks and put into a large bowl. Add the buttery garlic and chard mixture. Toss lightly to combine and evenly distribute all the ingredients.

3 For the dressing, mix together the olive oil and lemon juice. Pour over the bread and chard mixture, then leave to sit for 20 minutes in the fridge to give all the flavours a chance to combine.

4 Just before serving, toss through the mozzarella, herbs and pine nuts. Season and serve, preferably when you are holidaying in Italy!

BROAD BEAN

QUINOA AND FETA SALAD

The lively zing of the parsley and limes in this salad sits nicely with the taste of salty feta and sweet beans. Quinoa makes this a filling meal, but you could also use rice, couscous or pearl barley.

SERVES 4–6 – PREP TIME: 25 MINUTES
COOK TIME: 15 MINUTES

400g broad beans
150g quinoa
a large knob of butter
75g flaked almonds
150g feta cheese, crumbled

For the parsley dressing
1 large garlic clove
3 tablespoons extra virgin olive oil
25g bunch of flat-leaf parsley
juice and zest of 2 unwaxed limes

1 Prepare your broad beans by bringing a pan of water to the boil and dropping the beans in for 4–5 minutes, until just tender, before draining them and running under cold water. You should now be able to slip off the tough grey coats of the beans and reveal the bright green inner bean (this stage isn't necessary but it makes a superior salad). Set the beans aside.

2 Meanwhile, cook the quinoa, tipping it into a pan of boiling water and simmering gently for about 8 minutes, until it is soft but still has a little bite. Drain and set aside.

3 Make the dressing by blitzing the garlic, olive oil, parsley and lemon juice to create a gorgeous green consistency. Add a touch of water if the dressing needs loosening or if your limes are particularly dry. The easiest tool for this is a hand-held blender, but you can also chop the parsley finely and mix it with the other dressing ingredients. Stir through the lemon zest.

4 Heat the butter in a small frying pan over a medium heat, add the almonds and toast until just beginning to brown. In a big bowl mix the broad beans, quinoa, buttered almonds, feta (keeping a little aside for garnish) and the parsley dressing. Serve on a platter and top with a little more crumbled feta.

FRENCH BEANS

AND ALMONDS IN A BLUE CHEESE DRESSING

My mother has always said that there is no point going to the hairdresser if no one can tell afterwards whether you've had your hair cut. I feel the same way about dressings. If you go through the effort to create one, make sure your guests taste the results! This modern take on retro blue cheese dressing is the making of this dish using French beans.

SERVES 6 – PREP TIME: 12 MINUTES
COOK TIME: 10 MINUTES

50g flaked almonds
400g French beans, trimmed
sea salt and freshly ground
 black pepper

For the dressing
70g creamy Gorgonzola or other soft blue cheese
50ml natural yogurt
1 small garlic clove, crushed
½ tablespoon cider vinegar
½ teaspoon Dijon mustard

1 Begin by making your dressing – combine all the ingredients in a jug with 2 tablespoons water and blitz using a hand-held blender (alternatively mix in the small attachment of a food-processor). The resulting dressing should be lovely and thick.

2 Heat a dry frying pan over a medium heat and add the almonds. Watching carefully, toast the nuts for 2–3 minutes until they are beautifully golden. Set aside.

3 Bring a large pan of salted water to the boil and add the beans. Reduce the heat and simmer for about 5 minutes until just tender. Err towards undercooking rather than overcooking as it's lovely to have some crunch.

4 Drain the beans and immediately run under cold water to stop the cooking process. Tip the beans into a bowl and pour over the dressing and three-quarters of the toasted almonds. Season with salt and black pepper. Transfer to a serving dish and scatter with the remaining almonds.

BROAD BEAN

AND HERB FRITTATA

When I was a child, broad beans were a staple during the summer months, served hot in a parsley sauce. I remember not liking them much, finding the taste a little bitter and their grey coats a little tough. It was only years later I learnt that broad beans could be podded. They shed their bitter skins and reveal a young, beautiful bright green inner bean. This frittata transforms the old, grey beans into a wonderfully young and appetising dinner in hardly any time at all.

SERVES 3–4 – PREP TIME: 20 MINUTES
COOK TIME: 20 MINUTES

300g broad beans
2 tablespoons olive oil
6 spring onions, sliced
6 large free-range eggs
2 tarragon leaves, chopped
2 tablespoons chopped flat-leaf parsley

40g grated Parmesan or pecorino cheese, or a
 vegetarian-friendly alternative
salt and freshly ground black pepper
fresh tomato salad, to serve

20cm non-stick ovenproof frying pan

1 Bring a medium saucepan of water to the boil and add the beans. Allow them to simmer for 5 minutes, until they are just tender. Drain well before popping the bright green beans from their grey skins. This might seem a little laborious but will improve both the look and taste of the final dish.

2 Preheat the grill to high. Heat a little of the oil in the non-stick frying pan and add the spring onions. Fry for a minute or two, until just soft. Remove from the heat.

3 Crack the eggs into a medium bowl and add the podded broad beans, spring onions, tarragon, parsley and cheese. Season the mixture with salt and black pepper.

4 Return the non-stick frying pan to a medium/low heat and add the remaining olive oil. When hot, pour in the egg mixture. Leave to cook, without stirring, until the bottom has set.

5 Move the frittata to the grill and cook the top for a few minutes, until it is puffed and slightly golden. Serve straight away with a fresh tomato salad.

tip! *A non-stick pan is essential to prevent any expletives when trying to slide the frittata out!*

SWEETCORN
AND CHERRY TOMATO FRITTERS

My friend Alice is the kindest and most generous soul. We have had many adventures together, shared too many conversations and discussed food endlessly as if it was a master's art. She is an extraordinary cook and I admire her greatly. This recipe was prompted by an Alice idea; I've just juggled with it a little. The fritters are lovely, light and delicious scattered with rock salt.

MAKES 10 – PREP TIME: 15 MINUTES
COOK TIME: 15 MINUTES

300g cherry tomatoes, halved
2 tablespoons pesto
3 medium free-range eggs, separated
2 tablespoons chopped basil
150g sweetcorn kernels
175g self-raising flour

2 tablespoons vegetable oil, for frying
rock salt, to serve
4 tablespoons crème fraîche, to serve
a few basil leaves, roughly chopped, to garnish
salt and freshly ground black pepper

1 To make the fritters, place the cherry tomatoes in a large bowl and scrunch with your hands until lightly crushed and very juicy. Stir in the pesto, egg yolk, basil and sweetcorn. Season. Gradually stir in the flour to form a thick batter.

2 In a separate, clean bowl whisk the egg white to stiff peaks. Gently fold through the batter.

3 Heat the oil in a large frying pan over a medium-high heat. When the oil is hot but not smoking, drop spoonfuls of the fritter mixture into the pan. Fry for 3–4 minutes, turning halfway, until puffed up and golden. Using a slotted spoon, remove to a plate lined with kitchen paper. Cook in batches to prevent overcrowding and keep the cooked fritters warm in a low oven.

4 Sprinkle with rock salt and more freshly ground black pepper and serve with some crème fraîche and chopped basil.

FENNEL

AND MELON WITH MINT AND HONEY DRESSING

The fennel heads that gladden our food markets in early spring need little work and make an excellent ingredient, simply sliced razor thin and served raw.

SERVES 4
PREP TIME: 20 MINUTES

1 medium fennel bulb
¼ honeydew melon
¼ Galia melon
75g black olives
¼ cucumber, sliced
a small bunch of mint, leaves finely chopped, leaving some aside for garnish
2 teaspoons poppy seeds
zest of 1 unwaxed orange, to garnish

For the dressing
juice of 1 orange
2 tablespoons extra virgin olive oil
1 tablespoon runny honey
salt and freshly ground black pepper

1 Prepare the fennel by slicing it in half and carefully making a triangular-shaped cut around the firm core at the base. Remove the core and discard. Slice the remaining flesh on a mandolin or thinly slice with a sharp knife. Tip the fennel into a large bowl.

2 Remove any seeds from the melons and cut the flesh away from the skin. Slice into small chunks and add to the fennel with the olives, sliced cucumber, chopped mint and poppy seeds.

3 Make the dressing by briskly whisking the orange juice, olive oil and runny honey with a little salt and black pepper. Pour the dressing over the salad and gently toss with your hands to combine. Mound onto a serving plate, garnished with orange zest and a little more fresh mint.

FENNEL

PEAR AND STAR ANISE JAM

Fennel and star anise work well together, with flavours reminiscent of black liquorice. As the fennel, spice, pears, shallot, brown sugar and vinegar simmer they gently meld to a delicious combination of sweet and sour. Store in jars and bring out with bread and wedges of blue cheese.

MAKES 4 JARS
PREP TIME: 45–50 MINUTES
COOK TIME: 1 HOUR 40 MINUTES

2 tablespoons olive oil
600g fennel bulbs (about 2), trimmed and very thinly sliced
2 large banana shallots, thinly sliced
4 ripe pears (about 600g), peeled and cored with the flesh cut into 2–3cm cubes
6 garlic cloves, sliced
2 star anise
300ml cider vinegar
200g soft brown sugar
4cm piece of ginger, peeled and finely chopped
2 teaspoons fennel seeds, lightly crushed
2 teaspoons coriander seeds, lightly crushed
sea salt

1 Heat the olive oil in a large saucepan over a medium heat. Add the fennel and shallots and sprinkle with a little salt. Cook, covered, for about 15 minutes, until the fennel and onions have softened, stirring every so often.

2 Stir through the pear chunks and garlic and cook, this time uncovered, for a further 30 minutes. The consistency at this stage will have thickened up and be slightly jammy.

3 Mix in the remaining ingredients and continue to simmer over a medium heat for an hour longer, stirring regularly to prevent the jam catching on the base of the pan. Allow the jam to cool slightly before spooning it into 4 × 250ml sterilised jars (you can sterilise jars in the dishwasher – simply put on a high temperature setting). The jam will keep for up to year in properly sterilised jars.

CHICORY

PEAR, DATE AND POMEGRANATE SALAD

*Plump dates are one of life's luscious treasures. Stalls in Morocco sell them by the bucket load in varying quality –
the cheapest seem to lack a little body but the more you are prepared to pay, the more astonishing they become.
Dates are my vice. I'd choose them over chocolate and cook with them often. Needless to say, they were my
starting point for this salad and seem to sit perfectly with bitter, fresh chicory.*

SERVES 4 – PREP TIME: 25 MINUTES

1 pomegranate
1 head chicory, sliced and separated into
    single pieces
16 plump dates, stones removed and each
    cut in half
3 tablespoons roughly chopped flat-leaf parsley
1 ripe pear, cored and sliced

For the dressing
1 teaspoon runny honey
3cm piece of ginger, peeled and finely grated,
    juices and all
a pinch of ground cinnamon
juice of 1 large lemon

1 Deseed the pomegranate and place the seeds in a large bowl. My tip for this is to submerge the pomegranate under cold water to prevent lots of mess. Simply score the bright red skin and pull apart the fruit. Working beneath the surface of the water and using your fingers, prise the seeds away from the husk. The seeds will sink to the bottom of the water and any excess membranes will float.

2 Make your dressing by mixing together all the ingredients. Set aside while you assemble the salad.

3 Gently toss the chicory leaves with the dates, pomegranate seeds and chopped parsley. Add the pear slices to the bowl.

4 Pour the dressing over the salad and gently toss to combine before piling onto a platter.

RADISHES

WITH WHIPPED RICOTTA

This simple dip tastes glorious. The secret is to use a good-quality
Italian ricotta – this will make all the difference.

SERVES 4 AS A DIP – PREP TIME: 5 MINUTES

100g cream cheese
250g ricotta
zest of 1 unwaxed lemon

sea salt
a good glug of olive oil
a bunch of pink radishes

1 Tip the cream cheese and ricotta into a bowl. Beat for 5 minutes with a wooden spoon until light. Dollop on a plate and top with fresh lemon zest, sea salt and lashings of olive oil. Serve with crunchy fresh radishes.

CHICORY

APPLE AND HAZELNUT FREEKEH

Meet freekeh, the Middle Eastern grain that is very easy to cook, stacked full of protein and has an unusual smoky taste (once picked, the wheat is roasted over fire to burn away the husks). It is becoming widely available and is worth seeking out as an interesting ingredient. It might just become the new robust, staple grain in your cupboard.

SERVES 6 – PREP TIME: 25 MINUTES
COOK TIME: 20 MINUTES

185g wholegrain freekeh
1 head chicory, leaves chopped, stem sliced
1 large green apple, cored and finely sliced
75g hazelnuts with skins, roughly chopped
1 celery stick, finely sliced
½ bunch of flat-leaf parsley, finely chopped
salt and freshly ground black pepper

warm, buttered bread, to serve

For the dressing
2 small garlic cloves, crushed
3–4 tablespoons extra virgin olive oil
juice of ½ lemon
1 tablespoon cider vinegar

1 Bring a medium pan of water to the boil and add the freekeh. Bring back to the boil, then cover the pan and reduce the heat to low. Simmer for 15–20 minutes, or until the grains are al dente. Drain the excess water and set aside.

2 Get your dressing ready by whisking together (or vigorously shaking in a sealed jar) the crushed garlic, olive oil, lemon juice and cider vinegar. Taste and adjust according to your palate – this is the moment to trust your own opinion.

3 Keeping a few hazelnuts back for garnish, put all the prepared ingredients in the largest mixing bowl you have and gently toss them together. Sprinkle with salt and pepper. Tip into a serving bowl and spoon over the dressing. Sprinkle the remaining hazelnuts over the dish and serve with warm, buttered bread, if you want.

tip! *The cooked grain keeps for well over a week in the fridge, so I'll often cook more than I need for a particular recipe just so I have extra to hand to stir into soups or salads during the week.*

CHARD

This is a flavourful and wonderfully easy idea for a lunch on the move. Chard is perfect but you can substitute cabbage, spinach or kale if they are easier to find. The trick is waiting until the Stilton has melted, just enough to slightly 'stick' the mixture together, then you can just roll the wraps up and eat them – it's like an edible Tupperware!

MAKES 3 WRAPS – PREP TIME: 10 MINUTES
COOK TIME: 20 MINUTES

a small glug of olive oil
a knob of butter
1 small red onion, finely chopped
2 garlic cloves, finely chopped
¼ teaspoon crushed dried chilli
100–120g chard, stems discarded and leaves
     roughly chopped
small (210g) can butter or cannellini beans,
     drained and rinsed
50g Stilton cheese, crumbled
4 tablespoons soured cream
3 large wraps, flatbreads or tortillas
salt and freshly ground black pepper

❶ Heat the oil and butter in a large sauté pan. Cook the red onion, garlic and dried chilli over a low-medium heat for 8–10 minutes, stirring occasionally until golden and soft. Add the chard leaves and cook for a further 3–4 minutes, until wilted. Season well with salt and pepper.

❷ Stir the beans and crumbled Stilton into the chard mixture and heat through for a few minutes, until the Stilton has just begun to melt into the mixture to pull it together.

❸ Spread the soured cream down the centre of each wrap and then top with the chard mixture. Tuck in the ends and fold or roll into a wrap.

RADISH

I feel virtuous when I eat this salad, as if it might undo the previous night's antics or catapult me into a size 10. Peppery, pink radishes are so beautiful and set against pale ribbon noodles they make a light dinner or an unusual but welcome picnic lunch.

SERVES 4 – PREP TIME: 30 MINUTES
COOK TIME: 3–4 MINUTES

150g flat rice noodles
150g broad beans (or 100g soya beans)
150g pink radishes, thinly sliced
1 red chilli, deseeded and chopped
1 large, firm avocado, destoned and cut into slices
a good handful of mint, chopped, plus a sprig
     to garnish
a few tablespoons of nigella (or black sesame seeds)

For the dressing
2 tablespoons sesame oil
zest and juice of 2 unwaxed limes,
     reserving some to garnish
1 teaspoon caster sugar
6cm piece of ginger, peeled and finely grated
1 tablespoon fish sauce

❶ Put the rice noodles and broad beans into a large bowl and pour over boiling water. Allow to sit for 4–5 minutes, or until tender, before draining. Pod the broad beans to reveal their bright green insides.

❷ Add the radishes, chilli, avocado and mint to the noodles and podded beans. Toss everything together until well mixed.

❸ Make the dressing by combining all the ingredients in a small bowl. Pour the dressing over your salad and scatter with the seeds. Serve, garnished with a fresh sprig of mint and lime zest.

FRUITS OF THE EARTH

When I look at this collection I can't help but be drawn to the structure of these savoury fruits. The beautiful, soft, flavoursome skin gives way to the softer texture of flesh before encountering the chewiness or sometimes crunchiness of the seeds. There is so much going on in each perfect package that they can simply stand alone as a plate by themselves.

TOMATO

COBBLER

Some combinations seem not to like reinvention, and cheese and tomato falls firmly into that category. So I haven't reinvented them, and I think this is one of the best recipes in the book. Serve with a crisp green salad.

SERVES 4–6 – PREP TIME: 30 MINUTES
COOK TIME: 1 HOUR 15 MINUTES

2 tablespoons olive oil
3 medium onions, finely sliced
1kg tomatoes, roughly chopped
1 tablespoon fresh thyme leaves (or 1 teaspoon
    dried thyme), plus extra for the topping
1 tablespoon brown sugar
4 garlic cloves, crushed
salt and freshly ground black pepper

For the cobbler
300g self-raising flour
150g salted butter, softened
50g Cheddar cheese, finely grated
1 free-range medium egg, plus 1 egg yolk, beaten
a few drops of milk, if needed
green salad, to serve

2-litre ovenproof dish

1 Heat the oil in a large frying pan over a medium heat and add the onions. Reduce the heat to low and gently fry for at least 20 minutes (if you have the time, cook for another 10 minutes as they will keep improving), stirring every so often to make sure they don't catch. The onions will become soft, golden and almost sticky.

2 Meanwhile, preheat the oven to 190°C/170°C fan/ gas mark 5.

3 Make your cobbler dough by putting the flour into a large bowl and adding the butter. Using your fingertips, rub the two together until the butter has all but disappeared. Add the Cheddar and a generous serving of black pepper and mix them in. Pour in the beaten egg and bring everything together to form a soft dough, adding a drop or two of milk, if needed. Leave your cobbler for a few moments while you finish the filling.

4 Add the tomatoes, thyme, brown sugar and crushed garlic to the sticky onion and cook for 3–4 minutes over a medium heat. The tomatoes will just begin to soften. Remove from the heat at this point; you don't want them to break down, simply to start the cooking process.

5 Season the tomato mixture with a little salt and pepper and pour into a 2-litre ovenproof dish. Crumble over the cobbler topping, top with a few extra thyme leaves and bake for 40 minutes.

tip! *The tomatoes could range from cherry tomatoes to beef tomatoes to yellow tomatoes.*

TOMATO

AND PUY LENTIL LASAGNE

One and a half kilos of tomatoes are squeezed into this recipe, juice, skin, seeds and all. They are gently roasted so a little of the moisture cooks away but the flavour becomes all the more intense. Only make this in the summer while tomatoes are in season, at their best and are reasonably priced.

SERVES 6 – PREP TIME: 25 MINUTES
COOK TIME: 2 HOURS 15 MINUTES

1.5kg ripe red tomatoes, gently washed
2 tablespoons olive oil
2 tablespoons finely chopped rosemary
5 large garlic cloves, finely chopped
250g ready cooked Puy lentils
250g fresh lasagne

300g full fat crème fraîche
60g Parmesan cheese
sea salt and freshly ground black pepper
green salad, to serve

2-litre ovenproof dish

1 Preheat your oven to 130°C/110°C fan/gas mark 1. To prepare the tomatoes, cut each one in half horizontally and then each half into 4 chunks.

2 Lay the tomatoes on an enormous baking tray or divide them between two trays. Trickle over the olive oil and sprinkle over the chopped rosemary and garlic. Season well with sea salt and black pepper and give the whole lot a good stir. Put in the oven for 1½ hours.

3 When the tomatoes are done, remove them from the oven. Using a potato masher, gently mash the tomatoes until the flesh has almost disintegrated and you are left with the juicy flesh and skins. Transfer this tomato mixture to a bowl and stir it into the lentils. Season well.

4 Increase the oven temperature to 180°C/160°C fan/gas mark 4. Construct your lasagne by pouring roughly a third of the tomato lentil mixture into a 2-litre ovenproof dish. Top with the fresh pasta, then dollop with a third of the crème fraîche and a sprinkling of Parmesan. Cover with a second third of the tomato lentil mixture. Top with fresh lasagne sheets and crème fraîche. Repeat the process until all the mixture has been used up. Finish with fresh pasta on the top layer with enough crème fraîche to slather over the top.

5 Grate over a generous amount of Parmesan and a lovely grinding of black pepper. Place on the middle shelf of the oven and cook for 45 minutes. Serve with a fresh green salad.

ROASTED
TOMATOES
WITH KOHLRABI, MINT AND SUNFLOWER SEEDS

You might not have heard of the vegetable kohlrabi, which means, 'cabbage turnip'. They are sweet and surprisingly juicy and really fresh when used in an autumnal salad. This dish works just as well warm as at room temperature, so is ideal for prepare-ahead lunches.

SERVES 4 – PREP TIME: 15 MINUTES
COOK TIME: 15 MINUTES

350g cherry tomatoes
1 tablespoon olive oil
100g bulgar wheat
150g kohlrabi
2 little gem lettuces, finely sliced
a handful of mint, roughly chopped
75g feta cheese, crumbled, reserving a little
  to garnish

salt and freshly ground black pepper
30g sunflower seeds, toasted, to garnish

For the dressing
3 tablespoons extra virgin olive oil
1 tablespoon white wine vinegar
1 teaspoon runny honey

1 Preheat the oven to 200°C/180°C/gas mark 6. Empty the whole cherry tomatoes onto a baking tray and drizzle over the oil. Toss until they are evenly coated, season and put in the oven for 10–15 minutes until they are soft and beginning to split.

2 Meanwhile bring a small saucepan of water to the boil. Add the bulgar wheat and simmer for 10–12 minutes. Drain and set aside.

3 Prepare the kohlrabi by removing any leaves, peeling any tough skin and cutting the flesh into matchstick-sized slivers using a julienne peeler or a sharp knife. Toss with the little gem lettuce and chopped mint. Add half the crumbled feta.

4 Mix together all the ingredients for the dressing.

5 Combine the bulgar wheat with the kohlrabi mix and pour over the dressing. Toss until all the ingredients are coated, adding a little more dressing if needed.

6 Transfer the bulgar wheat and kohlrabi mix to a large salad plate and add the hot tomatoes. Lightly toss the dish before serving in a generous pile, garnished with the remaining feta and sunflower seeds.

tip!

A great substitute for kohlrabi are broccoli stems, so don't throw them away!

CUCUMBER

BROWN RICE AND MISO SALAD

Cucumber, while best known for being partnered with cream cheese, is also capable of being elevated to great culinary heights.

SERVES 4 – PREP TIME: 20 MINUTES
COOK TIME: 30–35 MINUTES

150g brown rice
1 whole cucumber
1 red chilli, halved and very finely chopped
a small bunch of coriander, roughly chopped, reserving some to garnish
3 spring onions, finely sliced at an angle

For the dressing
2cm piece of ginger, peeled and finely grated
juice of ½ lemon
2 tablespoons miso paste
2 tablespoons extra virgin olive oil
1 tablespoon caster sugar
2 tablespoons sesame oil

1 Brown rice takes longer than you might think, so cook this first according to the pack instructions – this normally takes about 30 minutes.

2 Meanwhile, prepare your cucumber by slicing it in half lengthways and scooping out the soft seeds with a teaspoon, leaving you with a 'cucumber boat'. Using your best knife skills, slice the flesh finely and at an angle to produce crescent shapes. Tip into a large bowl and combine with the chopped red chilli, coriander and spring onions.

3 Make the dressing by putting all the ingredients into a jar with a lid and shaking them vigorously.

4 Drain the rice and rinse with warm water. Stir through the dressing before adding the cucumber mixture. Serve, garnished with a few coriander leaves.

AUBERGINE

MUNG BEAN AND MINT SALAD

This salad packs quite a punch and I hope you will enjoy it.

SERVES 4–6 – PREP TIME: 30 MINUTES PLUS 2 HOURS SOAKING
COOK TIME: 50 MINUTES

125g dried green mung beans, soaked for 1–2 hours
2 large aubergines, each cut into 16 'finger' shapes
4 tablespoons olive oil
1 teaspoon cumin seeds
100g pumpkin seeds, toasted
100g feta cheese
a small bunch of mint, finely chopped
salt and freshly ground black pepper

For the dressing
3 fat garlic cloves, well crushed
pinch of salt
pinch of sugar
1 tablespoon Dijon mustard
1 tablespoon tamarind paste
juice of 2 medium limes
1 tablespoon fish sauce
1 tablespoon boiling water

1 Rinse the mung beans and tip into a pan, cover with water and simmer for 40–50 minutes or until just tender, adding a little more water if necessary. Drain and set aside.

2 Preheat the oven to 200°C/180°C fan/gas mark 6. Spread the aubergine in a roasting tray with 3 tablespoons of the olive oil and the cumin seeds and season well. Give everything a good jumble and roast for 25 minutes.

3 Meanwhile, put all the ingredients for the dressing into a jar and shake well. Taste a little and adjust as you see fit, adding a little more sugar or lime juice.

4 Toast the pumpkin seeds in a dry frying pan over a high heat, for 2–3 minutes until their skins begin to burst.

5 Mix the aubergine, mung beans and half the pumpkin seeds, feta and mint. Stir through the dressing gently and garnish with the remaining seeds, feta and mint.

AUBERGINE

PARMIGIANA

Europeans once thought aubergines, like tomatoes, were poisonous, such is their exotic appearance. Thankfully the culinary potential of both these fruits, which are surprisingly similar, has since been discovered. Both have an edible, smooth skin, numerous soft seeds and firm flesh. This dish uses aubergine slices that are set to rest with intensely flavoured tomatoes and lashings of Parmesan. We ate this particular dish two nights in a row on a trip to Naples and would have done so again, but we had to catch our flight home.

SERVES 4–6 – PREP TIME: 20 MINUTES, PLUS 1–2 HOURS SALTING
COOK TIME: 2 HOURS

3 aubergines, sliced horizontally into 1cm slices
2–3 teaspoons sea salt
100ml olive oil
50g Parmesan cheese, finely grated
a bunch of basil, leaves picked

For the tomato sauce
60ml olive oil
1 red onion, finely chopped
1 tablespoon chopped flat-leaf parsley
1 tablespoon chopped basil
3 × 400g cans Italian chopped tomatoes

2-litre ovenproof dish

1 Layer the aubergine slices in a dish, baking sheet or a couple of colanders and sprinkle with salt. Leave for 1–2 hours. The salt will draw out the moisture and remove any bitterness. Pat the slices dry with kitchen paper – there is no need to wash the salt away.

2 To make the tomato sauce, heat the oil in a large pan and gently fry the onion until soft and almost golden. Add the chopped herbs and stir for a minute before adding the tomatoes. Season well, then cover and cook over a very low heat for an hour, stirring occasionally.

3 Preheat the oven to 220°C/200°C fan/gas mark 7. Generously brush each aubergine slice with olive oil and place them in a single layer on a baking tray (or two). Cook on the low shelves for 10 minutes, then turn over and cook for a further 5–10 minutes until they are golden. Reduce the oven to 180°C/160°C fan/gas mark 4.

4 Arrange the aubergine slices in a 2-litre dish and spoon over some tomato sauce. Sprinkle over a little Parmesan and fresh basil. Repeat the layers and return to the hot oven for 30–35 minutes until the top is crispy and the aubergine is soft.

tip! *It really is worth salting the aubergine slices – while it is tempting to ignore this instruction it does make a difference! Not only do you draw out any bitter notes in the aubergine, but also the slices will soak up less oil.*

AUBERGINE

AND YOGURT MOUSSAKA

This delightful moussaka simply involves layering aubergine, tomato and potato with one or two other Greek accents. It's a sumptuous dish fit for mythical gods and goddesses on a mere mortal budget.

SERVES 8 – PREP TIME: 30 MINUTES
COOK TIME: 1 HOUR 10 MINUTES

500–600g potatoes, peeled and cut into
    5mm slices
2 medium aubergines, sliced into 5mm–1cm rounds
3 tablespoons vegetable oil

For the tomato sauce
1 tablespoon olive oil
1 medium onion, roughly chopped
2 garlic cloves, finely sliced
1 teaspoon dried oregano
2 × 400g cans chopped tomatoes
2 tablespoons tomato purée

85g feta cheese, crumbled
1 vegetable stock cube, crumbled
a handful of fresh basil leaves, torn
salt and freshly ground black pepper

For the yogurt sauce
1 large free-range egg (or 2 medium ones), beaten
250ml full-fat Greek yogurt
freshly grated nutmeg
freshly grated Parmesan cheese

2-litre ovenproof dish

1 Preheat the oven to a hot 220°C/200°C fan/ gas mark 7. Bring a medium saucepan of water to the boil and add the potatoes, cooking for 5–6 minutes to take the edge off them. Drain.

2 Add the potatoes and aubergines to a large roasting tin or two smaller ones. Drizzle over the vegetable oil and toss the vegetables until lightly coated. Roast in the oven for 20 minutes until the aubergines have relaxed and are turning golden. Remove the roasting tin from the oven and reduce the oven temperature to 180°C/160°C fan/ gas mark 4.

3 Meanwhile start on the tomato sauce. Heat the oil in a large pan over a medium heat and add the onion, garlic and oregano and fry for 3–4 minutes, until just soft. Add the chopped tomatoes, tomato purée, feta and stock cube and simmer for about 10 minutes. Season to taste, remove from the heat and stir through the basil.

4 Lightly grease the 2-litre ovenproof dish and line the base with a third of the roasted aubergine and potato slices. Add half of the tomato mixture and repeat, finishing with a layer of potato and aubergine.

5 Make the yogurt sauce by combining the eggs, Greek yogurt and nutmeg in a small bowl. Pour this on top of your dish, spreading it out with a spatula. Sprinkle with Parmesan and cook for 45 minutes until the top is golden and the sauce is bubbling underneath trying to escape.

 tip! *Choose smooth, firm and shiny aubergines – just as with people, wrinkles or a dull appearance in an aubergine are a sign of old age or seriously hard living!*

PUMPKIN

KIBBE

A traditional dish popular in the Lebanon, Syria and Egypt, kibbe is a grain mixture based on bulgar wheat that is often made into patties and filled with meat or vegetables.

MAKES 12 – PREP TIME: 35–40 MINUTES PLUS 1 HOUR COOLING AND RESTING
COOK TIME: 50 MINUTES

800g blue pumpkin or butternut squash, peeled
   and cut into 3cm cubes
250g fine bulgar wheat (if you can't find it, use
   coarse bulgar wheat but soak overnight)
100g plain flour, plus extra if needed
a good handful of mint, chopped
1 teaspoon smoked paprika
½ teaspoon sea salt
zest of 1 unwaxed lemon
vegetable oil, for frying
1 lemon, cut into wedges, or juice stirred through
   natural yogurt, to serve

For the stuffing
2 tablespoons olive oil
1 small onion, very finely chopped
1 teaspoon cinnamon
½ teaspoons ground cloves
1 teaspoon grated nutmeg
1 teaspoon ground cumin
100g can chickpeas, drained and roughly chopped
100g young leaf spinach
a small handful of flat-leaf parsley, finely chopped
100g feta, crumbled
salt and freshly ground black pepper

1 Put the pumpkin or squash in a medium saucepan and cover with cold water. Bring to the boil over a medium heat, then reduce the heat and simmer for 20–25 minutes, or until nicely softened. Drain and set aside to cool for about 20 minutes. Lightly mash with a potato masher.

2 Meanwhile, for the stuffing, heat the olive oil in a large frying pan over a medium heat, add the onion and cook until translucent. Stir through the spices and stir in the chickpeas, spinach, parsley and feta. Season and fry for a few minutes. Remove from the heat and let it cool.

3 Put the mashed pumpkin or squash in a large bowl with the raw bulgar, flour, mint, smoked paprika, salt and lemon zest. Gently mix together – you are looking for a dough-like consistency, but not as thick and dry. Set aside for 10 minutes to let the bulgar soften. If the dough appears dry, add a few drops of water and knead well. Add a little more flour, if needed, to create a more pliable

dough, then taste and add salt and more pepper, if liked. Place the pumpkin dough aside for 30 minutes to rest.

4 To shape the kibbe, roll the mixture into 24 × 40g balls, and use your thumb to make an indentation about 2cm deep. Fill a ball with a teaspoon of the filling and place another ball on top. Pinch all the way around to secure, then roll the kibbe into a lemon shape. Repeat until all the dough and filling are used. Set aside.

5 Heat the vegetable oil in a medium, heavy-based saucepan to 170°C (or until a cube of bread browns in 20 seconds). Add three or four kibbe at a time (so you don't overcrowd the pan) and cook for 3–4 minutes or until they are lightly golden and crisp. Remove with a slotted spoon and drain on kitchen paper.

6 Serve hot or at room temperature with mint, lemon yogurt or a squeeze of lemon juice.

PUMPKIN

TERRINE

This recipe is great for kick-starting a meal. Once the courgettes are cooked, it is just a question of fitting all the remaining ingredients in the tin and leaving the oven to do the hard work. Let the terrine sit for a short while to settle before slicing.

SERVES 6–8 – PREP TIME: 45 MINUTES
COOK TIME: I HOUR 20 MINUTES

2 long courgettes, thinly sliced lengthways
(you can use a mandolin)
olive oil, to grease
500g pumpkin flesh, peeled, deseeded and
cut into 7.5mm thin slices
70g rocket leaves, plus extra, to serve
75g cooked chestnuts, roughly chopped
75g blue cheese, crumbled

250ml double cream
2 medium free-range eggs, beaten
1 tablespoon Dijon mustard
20g Parmesan, finely grated
salt and freshly ground black pepper

900g/2lb loaf tin (23 × 13 × 7cm)

1 Brush the courgette slices with oil and then griddle (see tip) over a high heat for 1–2 minutes on each side, until golden and softened. Preheat oven to 160°C/140°C fan/gas mark 3. Brush the loaf tin with oil to lightly grease.

2 Lay the strips of courgette across the base and up the sides of the tin – don't worry about any overhang, this can be tidied away later. Finish each end with more charred strips, reserving some for the top.

3 Arrange a third of the pumpkin over the courgette and top with half the rocket, half the chestnuts and a third of the blue cheese. Season with salt and pepper. Make another layer using half of the remaining pumpkin. Top with the remaining rocket and chestnut and half of the remaining blue cheese. Season and then add a final layer of pumpkin.

4 Put the cream, egg, mustard, Parmesan and the remaining blue cheese in a medium bowl. Season and whisk gently until well combined. Pour the cream mixture over the pumpkin. Gently tap on the work surface to ensure the cream has run into any small holes. Fold over any overhanging courgette slices and then top with the remaining slices to cover.

5 Put on a baking tray and cook in the preheated oven for 1¼ hours or until the pumpkin is tender and the mixture is just set. Remove from oven and set aside for 15 minutes to cool slightly. Turn out onto a platter and use a serrated knife to cut into eight thick slices.

tip! *If you don't own a griddle pan, simply fry the courgette slices until they are a little charred.*

variation
You can replace the pumpkin with butternut squash.

PUMPKIN

PIE WITH CINNAMON MERINGUE

If you are not quite sure whether or not to make this recipe, let me help create it in your mind.
Imagine fluffy meringue and sweet maple syrup. Think fudgy pumpkin on a crisp ginger crust.
Visualise open fires and hot toddy. And envisage a pudding that's perfect for a celebration.

SERVES 10 – PREP TIME: 30 MINUTES PLUS 20 MINUTES CHILLING
COOK TIME: 45 MINUTES

For the crust
225g ginger biscuits
85g unsalted butter, melted

For the pie filling
500g pumpkin flesh, peeled, deseeded and
    cut into 3cm cubes
¼ teaspoon ground nutmeg
¼ teaspoon ground ginger
¼ teaspoon ground cinnamon
60ml maple syrup

60ml single cream
5 medium free-range egg yolks, beaten

For the meringue
165g caster sugar
3 medium free-range egg whites, at room
    temperature
½ teaspoon cinnamon
2 teaspoons corn flour

20cm loose-bottomed round flan tin

1 Preheat the oven to 180°C/160°C fan/gas mark 4. To make the pie crust, tip the biscuits into a blender or food-processor and process into small crumbs. Add the melted butter and mix well. Spoon the buttery biscuit mix into the flan tin and, using an oiled spatula or oiled fingers, push the mixture over the base and right up the sides to form a slanting edge. Chill the crust in the fridge for 20 minutes to harden up.

2 Place the tin on a baking sheet (this results in a more even bake) and bake in the preheated oven for 10–12 minutes. Remove from the oven and allow to cool slightly.

3 Meanwhile, bring a small pan of water to the boil and add the pumpkin cubes. Simmer for about 15 minutes until the flesh is tender and cuts like butter. Drain well and purée the pumpkin in a blender or food-processor. Mix the purée with the spices, maple syrup, cream and egg yolks. The mixture will be of quite a liquid consistency, so pour it into the crust and bake for 20–25 minutes until it is just set but with a slight wobble.

4 This recipe uses the Italian meringue method of cooking egg whites with hot sugar syrup to make a really voluminous topping. Put the sugar and 60ml water into a heavy saucepan and bring to the boil, stirring occasionally. If any sugar crystals stick to the side of the pan, brush them down into the syrup with a clean, wet brush. The syrup is ready when it reaches 120°C or when it solidifies when a small amount is dropped into a glass of cold water.

5 When the syrup has reached the right temperature, whisk the egg whites to stiff peaks with an electric hand whisk. Pour the syrup onto the whites in three stages, working as fast as possible and whisking hard after each addition. Add the cinnamon and corn flour and keep whisking until the mixture is cool. The meringue should be stiff and shiny. Dollop the meringue on the pie and flash it under a hot grill for 2–3 minutes; or, brown with a blowtorch before serving.

114

PUMPKIN

BANANA AND MAPLE CAKE

My sister Caroline told me that this is the best cake she has ever tasted. She helped me perfect the quantities; we both think the addition of ripe bananas is the secret. That, and a thick maple sweet icing slathered on the top.

SERVES 10 – PREP TIME: 25 MINUTES
COOK TIME: 1 HOUR

300g self-raising flour
300g light brown sugar
2 teaspoons cinnamon
2 teaspoons bicarbonate
 of soda
½ teaspoon salt
2 ripe bananas (about
 175g peeled)
3 medium free-range
 eggs, beaten
100g unsalted butter,
 melted

400g pumpkin flesh,
 grated
50g hazelnuts, toasted
 and roughly chopped,
 to decorate

For the icing
250g mascarpone
2 tablespoons icing sugar
3–4 tablespoons maple
 syrup

25cm square cake tin

1 Preheat the oven to 180°C/160°C fan/gas mark 4 and grease and line a 25cm square tin with baking parchment.

2 Put all the dry ingredients into a medium bowl and mix well. Next, take the biggest bowl you have and squish the bananas into a pulp with a potato masher or wooden spoon. Add in the eggs, melted butter and pumpkin flesh and give everything a good stir.

3 Add the dry mixture to the wet one, combining them well and pour the batter into the cake tin. Transfer to the middle shelf of the oven and bake for 55–60 minutes or until the centre of the cake springs back to the touch.

4 To make the icing, mix the mascarpone with a wooden spoon and gradually stir through the icing sugar and maple syrup. Spread generously onto the cooled cake and sprinkle with toasted, chopped hazelnuts.

AVOCADO

POPPYSEED AND ALMOND CAKE

Don't knock this until you've tried it. It makes perfect sense that the buttery, rich flesh of the avocado is glorious in a cake and negates the need for any butter.

MAKES 2 × 18CM CAKES – PREP TIME: 20 MINUTES
COOK TIME: 40 MINUTES

flesh of 2 small ripe
 avocados, about 250g
300g ground almonds
300g caster sugar
juice and zest of
 1 unwaxed lemon
3 medium free-range
 eggs, beaten
1 teaspoon baking
 powder

½ teaspoon bicarbonate
 of soda
1 tablespoon poppy seeds,
 plus extra to decorate

For the icing
125g cream cheese
300g icing sugar, sifted
50g unsalted butter

2 × 18cm cake tins

1 Preheat the oven to 180°C/160°C fan/gas mark 4 and grease and line the cake tins with baking parchment.

2 Put the avocado flesh into a blender or food-processor and add the ground almonds and sugar. Whizz until you have a gorgeous green paste.

3 Transfer the avocado mixture to a bowl and add the lemon juice zest and eggs, one element at a time, stirring the mixture well. Mix in the baking powder, bicarbonate of soda and poppy seeds until the seeds are evenly distributed. Spoon the mixture evenly into the cake tins and bake for 40 minutes until the cake is just firm to the touch. Remove from the oven and allow to cool on a wire rack.

4 Make the icing by beating the cream cheese and butter in a medium bowl to soften and, working quickly, whisk through the icing sugar. Use a palette knife to slather the icing over the cake and then top with poppy seeds.

tip! *If you would prefer to cook the cake in 2 × 20cm cake tins, add an extra egg to the mixture.*

SMASHED
AVOCADO
LIME AND REFRIED BEAN BURRITO

Choose your avocados carefully – the best ones are plump and dark green with just enough give in them to feel soft, not solid. Creamy avocado, sharp lime and spicy beans all wrapped up in a tortilla duvet – heaven?

MAKES 2 LARGE BURRITO – PREP TIME: 15 MINUTES
COOK TIME: 10 MINUTES

a glug of vegetable oil
2 garlic cloves, mashed
1 teaspoon ground cumin
¼ teaspoon chilli flakes
1 × 350–400g can black beans, drained
1 large ripe avocado, halved, stoned and peeled
2 tablespoons roughly chopped coriander
juice of 1 unwaxed lime
4 large tortillas
3 tablespoons soured cream
40g Cheddar cheese, finely grated

1 Heat the oil in a large saucepan over a medium heat and add the garlic, cumin and chilli flakes. Fry for a minute or two before adding the beans. Allow the beans to warm through before mashing them with a fork or potato masher. Don't be too aggressive; it's lovely to have a little texture. Set the beans aside.

2 Put the buttery avocado flesh into a small bowl and mash with a fork. Stir though the coriander and lime juice, reserving a little to go in the wrap.

3 To assemble the burrito, spread a little soured cream over each tortilla, pile in the beans followed by the smashed avocado and top with Cheddar and a little more fresh lime juice. Fold each burrito from the bottom up, one side in and then roll secure with the other side. Wrap each burrito in foil and hand them out for the ultimate meal on the go.

RED PEPPER
SHAKSHUKA

This is an Israeli recipe that is often eaten as a brunch dish – I think of it as a kind of pizza but one that doesn't involve waiting for dough to rise.

SERVES 3 – PREP TIME: 15 MINUTES
COOK TIME: 30 MINUTES

2 tablespoons olive oil
1 red chilli, deseeded and finely chopped
1 onion, finely chopped
3 medium red peppers, deseeded and sliced into thin strips
4 garlic cloves, roughly chopped
1 teaspoon ground cumin
1 teaspoon turmeric
pinch of saffron
1 × 400g can chopped tomatoes
3 medium free-range eggs
natural yogurt, to serve
flat-leaf parsley, roughly chopped, to serve
toasted pitta bread, to serve

1 Heat the oil in a deep frying pan until hot and add the red chilli and onion. Sizzle for 2–3 minutes until the onion has begun to soften. Add the peppers, garlic and spices. Maintain the heat and continue to fry, covered, for 10–12 minutes. You want the peppers to be soft but not to char.

2 Pour in the tomatoes and continue to simmer for a further 8 minutes, uncovered, until the mixture has thickened slightly.

3 Using a spoon, shape three slight 'holes' in your pepper mixture. Crack the eggs into these holes – it doesn't matter if the white seeps onto the surface of the mixture. Cover and cook until the yolks are just set, for about 10 minutes. Serve the dish on toasted pitta with the yogurt and parsley.

tip! *If your pan doesn't have an obvious lid, use a baking tray instead.*

OKRA

WITH BUTTERBEAN PURÉE

Many of us know okra as 'ladies fingers' or 'gumbo' and associate the soft, green seedpods with a gloopy curry, but think again; they are delicious just roasted in a hot oven with plenty of sea salt and olive oil. Dip them into a loose butterbean purée and you have yourself some gorgeous pre-dinner fodder.

**SERVES 6 AS A STARTER – PREP TIME: 15 MINUTES
COOK TIME: 20 MINUTES**

450g okra, cut in half lengthways
1 tablespoon olive oil
½ teaspoon sea salt
freshly ground black pepper

For the butterbean purée
4 tablespoons extra virgin olive oil
4 garlic cloves, finely chopped
zest and juice of 1 large unwaxed lemon
2 × 400g cans butterbeans, drained and rinsed
¼ teaspoon sea salt

1 Preheat the oven to 200°C/180°C fan/gas mark 6. In a large bowl lightly toss the okra with the olive oil, salt and plenty of black pepper. Spread onto a baking sheet in a single layer and roast for 15 minutes, or until the edges are just beginning to turn golden.

2 Meanwhile, make the butterbean purée. Heat the olive oil in a frying pan over a medium heat for a minute or two before reducing the heat to low and adding the garlic and lemon zest. Cook for 1–2 minutes before stirring through the butter beans, salt and plenty of pepper and warming through. Transfer the butter beans to a blender or food-processor and blend to a smooth purée. Squeeze in the lemon juice and blend again, adding a little warm water to achieve your desired consistency. Taste until you have the seasoning 'just so'.

3 Serve the roasted okra in a humble pile alongside a bowl of butterbean purée.

PEPPER

AND HALLOUMI BRIOCHE BUNS

These beautiful buttery brioche buns are one of my favourite things to eat, not least when they are stuffed with charred peppers and salty halloumi.

MAKES 8 BUNS – PREP TIME: 40 MINUTES PLUS 1 HOUR 45 MINUTES PROVING
COOK TIME: 35 MINUTES

45ml warm milk
7g fast-action dried yeast
3 tablespoons caster sugar
450g strong white bread flour
2 teaspoons fine salt
35g cold unsalted butter
2 medium free-range eggs, beaten
75g plain flour

1 large free-range egg yolk, beaten
1 tablespoon poppy seeds
handful of rocket, to serve

For the filling
3 red peppers, cut into quarters and deseeded
250g block of halloumi, sliced into eight
4 tablespoons cream cheese

1 To make the brioche rolls, pour 200ml warm water and the warm milk into a small bowl and sprinkle over the yeast and 1 tablespoon of the sugar. Stir to blend and allow to sit for about 5 minutes until the surface of the mixture is a little foamy. This proves your yeast is active.

2 Meanwhile, combine the bread flour, salt and the remaining sugar in a large bowl. Add the butter and rub this into the flour until the mixture resembles breadcrumbs.

3 Beat the eggs into the yeast mixture. Make a hole in the centre of the flour mixture and add the yeast and egg mixture. Mix well with a wooden spoon.

4 Put the plain flour on the work surface and drop the sticky dough mixture on top. Begin to knead the flour into the mixture until it is fully incorporated. Then continue to knead the dough for a good 10 minutes, adding a little more flour if necessary.

5 Place the dough in a clean, lightly oiled bowl, cover with clingfilm and allow it to sit in a warm spot for an hour, until doubled in size.

6 Using a sharp knife, slice the dough into eight pieces. Lightly flour your work surface and shape each piece into a round, roll shape and place on a greased baking tray. Lightly cover with a dry tea towel. Allow the buns to sit for a further 45 minutes, to grow a little larger. Preheat the oven to 200°C/180°C/gas mark 6.

7 Brush each bun with beaten yolk, sprinkle over some poppy seeds and bake for 10 minutes until gorgeous and golden and the base feels hollow when tapped.

8 To make the filling, rub the peppers in a little oil and place on a baking sheet. Cook for 18–20 minutes, in the hot oven at 200°C/fan 180°C/gas mark 6 until softened and just beginning to char.

9 Heat a griddle pan over a high heat. After a few minutes, add the halloumi slices and grill for 2–3 minutes on each side, or until golden brown and slightly charred.

10 To assemble the buns, slice them in half, spread with cream cheese and stuff with hot peppers, salad leaves and caramelised halloumi.

BUTTERNUT

WEDGES WITH ROSEMARY

Butternut squash is a real all-rounder; it is as comfortable sitting in a soup as in a curry. This recipe allows the butternut to sing, in wedges, all on its own. Add a simple hit of rosemary, orange and maple and our wedges are fit for lunch.

MAKES 6 LARGE WEDGES – PREP TIME: 10 MINUTES
COOK TIME: 35 MINUTES

1 butternut squash
1 tablespoon olive oil
2 tablespoons marmalade

1 large rosemary sprig, finely chopped
juice and zest of 1 unwaxed orange
cracked black pepper

1 Preheat the oven to 200°C/180°C fan/gas mark 6. Prepare the butternut squash by washing any dirt from the skin and slicing off the very top and very bottom.

2 Using a sharp knife and a steady hand, cut the squash into 6 long wedges. Scoop out the seeds and place the wedges on a baking tray. Brush with olive oil and roast for 25 minutes.

3 Meanwhile, heat the marmalade in a small pan over a medium heat for a minute to warm through. Add the rosemary and orange juice and bring to a simmer. Cook for 3–4 minutes and set aside.

4 Remove the squash from the oven and brush the marmalade mixture over the wedges. Return them to the oven for a further 10 minutes.

5 Serve, garnished with fresh orange zest and cracked black pepper.

BUTTERNUT

THYME AND BROWN BREAD PUDDING

This is a lovely, chunky, savoury bread and butter pudding, which, despite sitting neatly in the vegetarian bracket, will satisfy the appetite of any hardened carnivore. I like to serve this boldly with nothing more than a few salad leaves and a chilled glass of cider.

SERVES 4–6 – PREP TIME: 15 MINUTES
COOK TIME: 40 MINUTES

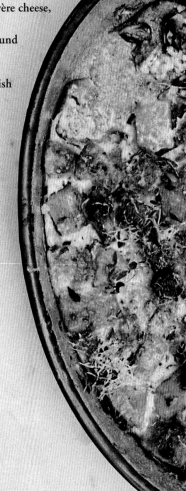

200g brown bread (roughly 4 thick slices, not pre-sliced), cut into 1.5cm cubes
½ large butternut squash (about 500g), peeled, deseeded and roughly cut into 1.5cm chunks
1 large red onion, roughly chopped
6 garlic cloves, sliced
a small bunch of thyme, leaves picked
4 tablespoons olive oil
1 teaspoon paprika

a little butter, for greasing
300ml crème fraîche
3 medium free-range eggs, beaten
3 tablespoons Gruyère cheese, finely grated
salt and freshly ground black pepper

2-litre ovenproof dish

1 Preheat the oven to 200°C/180°C fan/gas mark 6. Spread the bread cubes (crusts and all) on a large baking tray.

2 Add the butternut squash chunks to the baking tray, gently combining them with the bread. Add the chopped onion, sliced garlic and thyme. Drizzle over the olive oil and sprinkle with paprika. Give everything an enormous shake so all the ingredients are nicely muddled. Season generously with salt and pepper and bake for 20 minutes.

3 Grease the ovenproof dish. In a large bowl, mix the crème fraîche and the eggs until they are combined.

4 Once the squash and bread mixture has finished baking, and working quickly, tip everything into your crème fraîche and gently stir. Don't worry about making sure every bit is covered in mixture; it is quite nice to have a chunk or two without sauce.

5 Transfer the mixture into your waiting ovenproof dish. Sprinkle the Gruyère over the top. Reduce the oven temperature to 180°C/160°C fan/ gas mark 4 and bake for a further 20 minutes. Serve immediately.

BUTTERNUT

AND COCONUT SOUP

Celebrate the arrival of autumn with this glowing, silky soup. I've kept the flavours simple, allowing each one to sing for itself, but you can add fresh herbs, paprika or orange zest to spice things up to fit with your mood.

MAKES ENOUGH FOR 4 BOWLS – PREP TIME: 25 MINUTES
COOK TIME: 35 MINUTES

1 tablespoon olive oil
2 shallots, chopped
2 garlic cloves, crushed
1 large butternut squash, peeled, deseeded and
    cut into 3cm cubes

5cm piece of ginger, grated (add more if you want
    an extra hit of ginger)
a sprinkling of dried red chilli flakes, plus extra
    to garnish
200ml hot vegetable stock
400ml coconut milk, plus extra to garnish

1 Heat a large pan over a medium heat. Pour in the olive oil and heat for a moment or two before adding the shallots and garlic. Gently fry for 3–4 minutes until the shallots have softened. Then stir through the butternut cubes, ginger and chilli flakes.

2 Turn the heat down and sauté the butternut squash gently for 8–10 minutes, with the lid on. Stir regularly to prevent it catching on the bottom of the pan.

3 Remove the lid and pour over the hot vegetable stock and coconut milk. Bring the pan to a gentle simmer and cook for about 15–18 minutes, until the butternut squash is tender and cuts like soft butter.

4 Transfer the soup to a blender and blend until really smooth and silky. Return to the pan to heat through. Season to taste – it might take a few tastes to get this right. Serve in deep, warm bowls with a splattering of coconut milk and a few chilli flakes.

HIDDEN
BUTTERNUT
MAC AND CHEESE

Macaroni cheese is one of my childhood food gems. This dish elevates insignificant dried pasta into a brilliant recipe for children's tea. In this, my bright version, butternut, onion and garlic are blitzed beyond detection and served to unsuspecting youngsters.

SERVES 4 ADULTS OR 6 CHILDREN – PREP TIME: 40 MINUTES
COOK TIME: 15–20 MINUTES

300g dried macaroni
1 small butternut squash (around 600g), peeled, deseeded and cut into 1–2cm chunks
250ml hot vegetable stock
a knob of butter
1 onion, roughly chopped
2 garlic cloves, sliced

100ml semi-skimmed milk
1 teaspoon sea salt
65g mature Cheddar cheese, grated
a little chopped flat-leaf parsley
freshly ground black pepper

2-litre ovenproof dish

1 Preheat the oven to 200°C/180°C fan/gas mark 6. Lightly grease a 2-litre ovenproof dish with butter.

2 Put the macaroni on to cook. Bring a large pot of water to the boil, add the pasta and cook for 7–9 minutes until al dente, then drain well under running cold water and set aside.

3 Place the butternut squash in a small saucepan and pour over the hot vegetable stock. Simmer, covered, over a medium heat for 10–12 minutes until the squash cuts like butter.

4 Meanwhile, heat the butter in a small frying pan and add the onion and garlic. Fry over a medium heat for 4–5 minutes until just caramelised, and remove from the heat.

5 Add the onion and garlic to the softened butternut squash and stock. Pour over the milk and add the salt. Now blitz, ideally with a handheld blender.

6 Add the cooked macaroni to the mixture and stir until really well combined. Dollop the bright orange mix into your greased dish and top with grated cheese, chopped parsley and black pepper, in whichever order seems most natural. Bake for 15–20 minutes until the cheese is bubbling. Serve immediately.

MARROW

STUFFED WITH ORZO

Cooks and gardeners alike are often nervous of the marrow, such is its great volume, but fear not, marrow can taste good – even delicious. Here I've removed the watery flesh, chopped it, mixed it with orzo, plenty of garlic, flavourful tomatoes and fresh parsley, then returned the mix to the marrow shell and baked. The method is simple and the result is stacked with flavour.

SERVES 4 – PREP TIME: 10–15 MINUTES
COOK TIME: 35 MINUTES

1 marrow (around 600g in weight)
100g orzo pasta
1½ tablespoons olive oil
1 small onion, finely chopped
4 garlic cloves, finely chopped
100g pecorino cheese, finely grated
10 sun-dried tomato halves preserved in oil,
    drained and finely chopped

2 tablespoons pine nuts, toasted
a bunch of flat-leaf parsley, finely chopped
freshly ground black pepper

For the topping
4 tablespoons thick Greek yogurt
1 free-range egg, lightly beaten
a few pine nuts, to sprinkle

1 Preheat the oven to 180°C/160°C fan/gas mark 4. Cut the marrow in half horizontally. Carefully scrape the soft pulp out with a spoon, leaving a 1–1.5cm rim around the outside of the marrow. Roughly chop up the flesh and set aside.

2 Cook the orzo according to the pack instructions (for approximately 8 minutes). Drain and immediately rinse under cold water to stop the orzo cooking and toss with ½ teaspoon of the olive oil.

3 Heat a tablespoon of oil in a frying pan over a medium heat. Add the onion and garlic and fry for 3–4 minutes until the onion has softened.

4 Transfer the onion and garlic to a bowl and add the cooked orzo, pecorino, sun-dried tomatoes, pine nuts, parsley and marrow pulp. Season generously with black pepper. Mix well and then stuff the mixture into the marrow, squeezing it all in.

5 To make the topping, mix the yogurt and egg and spoon this over the filling. Sprinkle with pine nuts, place on a baking sheet and bake for 25 minutes.

COURGETTE

AND GOAT'S CHEESE PIZZA

¼ of the quantity of pizza dough below
6 tablespoons passata (see below)
olive oil, to grease
2 small courgettes, sliced into thin strips

150g goat's cheese, cut into thin slices
½ teaspoon dried chilli flakes
a handful of rocket leaves, to serve

1 Preheat the oven to 220°C/200°C/gas mark 7. Place a baking sheet in the oven to get really hot – this will ensure your pizza has a crisp base.

2 Knock back the dough by kneading it again for a minute or so. With a well-floured rolling pin, roll out the dough as thinly as possible. Remove the baking sheet from the oven and dust with flour before carefully

transferring the dough base onto it. Spread over a little of the passata, not more than necessary, about 6 tablespoons.

3 Brush the courgette strips with olive oil. Heat a griddle over a high heat and fry the strips until just charred; about 2 minutes on each side. Lay them over the passata with the goat's cheese slices and chilli flakes. Bake for 12–15 minutes. Sprinkle with rocket and serve.

PIZZA DOUGH

MAKES ENOUGH FOR 4 PIZZA BASES
PREP TIME: 30 MINUTES PLUS PROVING TIME

2 × 7g sachets fast-action dried yeast or 30g fresh yeast
2 teaspoons caster sugar
700g strong bread flour
2 teaspoons salt
50ml olive oil

1 Pour 180ml warm water into a small bowl and sprinkle over the yeast and sugar. Stir to blend and allow it to sit for about 5–10 minutes until the surface of the mixture is a little foamy. This proves your yeast is active.

2 Sift the flour and salt into a large bowl and make a well in the centre. Pour in the yeast mixture, the oil and another 180ml warm water. Mix well with your hands and add a little more flour if too wet or a touch more water if too dry.

3 Transfer the dough to a lightly floured surface and knead for about 8–10 minutes until soft and elastic. Return the dough to a clean, oiled bowl and cover with a damp tea towel or oiled clingfilm. Leave to rise somewhere warm for about 1½ hours until doubled in size.

TOMATO PASSATA

MAKES ENOUGH FOR 4 PIZZAS AND A PASTA DISH
PREP TIME: 30 MINUTES – COOK TIME: 1 HOUR 10 MINUTES

75ml olive oil
1 onion, finely chopped
2 tablespoons roughly chopped flat-leaf parsley
2 tablespoons roughly chopped basil
3 × 400g cans chopped tomatoes
1 teaspoon caster sugar
1 tablespoon red wine vinegar
salt and freshly ground black pepper

1 Heat the olive oil in a heavy-based saucepan over a medium heat. Add the onion and fry gently until it softens and turns almost golden. Add the herbs and fry for 30 seconds before carefully pouring in the tomatoes, then add the sugar and vinegar. Season well with salt and pepper, reduce the heat, and simmer your sauce, uncovered, for an hour. Stir occasionally to prevent anything catching on the bottom of the pan. At the end, season again with salt and pepper to taste.

COURGETTE

AND RICOTTA OMELETTE

*This is a beautiful way of making eggs fit for dinner.
Courgettes are not essential – you can replace them with
fresh peas, lightly steamed spinach or steamed beans.*

SERVES 1 – PREP TIME: 5 MINUTES
COOK TIME: 6 MINUTES

50g ricotta cheese
2 large free-range eggs,
  separated
2 small courgettes or
  1 larger one
2 tablespoons roughly
  chopped basil

2 tablespoons grated
  Parmesan cheese
a large handful of rocket
1 teaspoon butter
salt and freshly ground
  black pepper
green salad, to serve

1 Preheat the grill to high. Combine the ricotta, egg
yolks, courgette, basil and half of the Parmesan in a small
bowl. Season.

2 In a clean metal bowl, whisk the egg whites until they
stand in stiff peaks. Stir about a quarter of the egg white
and the rocket into the ricotta mixture, before gently
folding through the remaining egg white. Sprinkle over the
remaining Parmesan.

3 Heat the butter in a small frying pan and pour the
mixture into the pan. Gently fry over a medium heat for
3–4 minutes before putting the pan under the grill for
a final 2 minutes of cooking. Serve immediately with a
dressed green salad.

COURGETTE

SPAGHETTI WITH ROASTED TOMATOES

*This is a brilliant gluten-free recipe where ordinary spaghetti
is replaced by long strands of grated courgette cooked for just
a moment before being tossed with roasted cherry tomatoes.*

SERVES 2 – PREP TIME: 15 MINUTES
COOK TIME: 25 MINUTES

150g cherry tomatoes,
  (75g halved)
4 garlic cloves, sliced
1 small red chilli,
  deseeded and
  finely sliced
1 tablespoon olive oil
50g sunflower seeds

2 large courgettes, (the
  longer the better!)
1 free-range egg yolk
1 tablespoon thick
  Greek yogurt
a handful of basil,
  roughly chopped
plenty of salt and freshly
  ground black pepper

1 Preheat the oven to 200°C/180°C fan/gas mark 6. Put
the tomatoes, garlic and chilli into a small roasting tin and
drizzle over the olive oil. Shake well to coat and place in the
hot oven for 20 minutes.

2 Meanwhile, tip your sunflower seeds into a dry frying
pan and cook them over a medium heat for 3–4 minutes,
swirling the pan regularly. Remove from the heat once the
seeds have taken on some colour.

3 For the courgette spaghetti, lay a box grater on
its side and grate the length of the courgette into long
worms. Try not to be firm – a loose grip makes this easier.
Bring a medium saucepan of water to the boil and cook
the courgette strips for 1–2 minutes before draining in a
colander, gently squeezing out any excess water with the
back of a spoon. Return to the pan and stir through the egg
yolk followed by the yogurt. Season well.

4 Stir two-thirds of the roasted tomato mixture and
half of the sunflower seeds into the courgettes and divide
the mixture between two plates. Top with the remaining
tomatoes, toasted sunflower seeds, fresh basil and a good
seasoning of black pepper. Serve immediately.

COURGETTE

TOMATO & POLENTA TART

This recipe is a very informal version of a tart – it's a little bit messy, a mixture of courgettes, tomatoes and silky crème fraîche. The polenta base is unusual and, as well as ticking the 'gluten-free' box, it adds a wonderful texture and flavour, soaking up escaped juices from the tomatoes and becoming slightly crunchy at the edges. I like to have this with a friendly glass of wine and call it supper.

SERVES 4 – PREP TIME: 20 MINUTES
COOK TIME: 1 HOUR 10 MINUTES

For the polenta crust
500ml hot vegetable stock
140g polenta
1 tablespoon unsalted butter
50g Parmesan cheese, finely grated
1 free-range egg, lightly beaten
salt and freshly ground black pepper

For the tart
1 tablespoon olive oil
2 tablespoons crème fraîche
1 courgette, thinly sliced
2 medium tomatoes, sliced horizontally into
    thin slices
1 tablespoon thyme leaves, plus extra to garnish
25g Parmesan cheese, finely grated

21cm square tart tin

1 Start by making the polenta crust. Bring the vegetable stock to a simmer in a medium saucepan and pour the polenta into the water. Keep your pan over a low heat and, using a wooden spoon, stir the mixture constantly, thrashing out any lumps that try to form. Continue for around 6 minutes until the polenta is very thick – my advice would be to set a timer as it is easy to think you've done enough stirring at the 2 minute mark!

2 Remove the mixture from the heat and add the butter and Parmesan and stir until they have disappeared. Then stir through the beaten egg and a healthy seasoning of salt and pepper. Remove from the heat and allow the polenta to cool slightly.

3 Lightly grease the tart tin with olive oil. Put the polenta in the centre and, using a spatula or oiled fingers, gently tease it up the sides of the tin to create the sides of the crust.

4 Preheat the oven to 200°C/180°C fan/gas mark 6. Smother a thin layer of crème fraîche over the base of your tart and top with alternating slices of courgette and tomato. Finish with the thyme leaves and the Parmesan.

5 Cook on the middle shelf of the oven for 45 minutes. Reduce the temperature to 180°C/160°C fan/gas mark 4 and cook for a further 15 minutes. Remove and allow the tart to cool for 5–10 minutes to allow it to 'come to'. Serve in slices.

COURGETTE
CHOCOLATE AND PISTACHIO CAKE

I made this cake for three of my very best friends. Annabel, Rosanna and Amy joined me to spend the day walking on the South Downs. Despite a wrong turn, inappropriate walking shoes and not enough sustenance, we chatted and laughed our way to Brighton. Waiting for us was a cake I'd baked to celebrate our arrival. Black treacle and olive oil beaten into the mixture gives a gloriously fudgy cake, with the courgette adding a moist texture. I didn't think it was possible to feel so proud of a recipe but this one took many attempts to get just right and for that I do feel proud.

MAKES I × 20CM CAKE – PREP TIME: 25 MINUTES
COOK TIME: I HOUR 10 MINUTES

250g self-raising flour
2 small courgettes (around 250g), finely grated
60g cocoa powder
300g caster sugar
45g black treacle
150ml olive oil
3 medium free-range eggs, beaten

For the icing
100g chocolate (70% cocoa solids)
50g unsalted butter
75ml soured cream
125g icing sugar
35g pistachios, roughly chopped, to decorate

a deep 20cm cake tin

1 Preheat the oven to 180°C/160°C fan/gas mark 4 and put a baking tray on the middle shelf. Grease and line the cake tin with baking parchment.

2 Put the flour into a large bowl and add the courgettes, cocoa powder and caster sugar. Give everything a thorough mix. In a smaller bowl, gently beat the black treacle, olive oil and eggs. Combine the wet mixture with the dry mixture, stirring well with a wooden spoon. Pour the cake batter into your prepared tin.

3 Place the tin on the pre-warmed baking tray (this will ensure a lovely even heat) in the centre of the oven. Bake for between 1 hour and 1 hour 10 minutes until the centre of the cake springs back to the touch. Remove the cake from the oven and allow to cool in the tray.

4 To make the icing, melt the chocolate and butter in a bowl over a pan of gently simmering water. (Alternatively, melt in the microwave for 1 minute in which case watch it VERY carefully!) When melted, remove from the heat and stir in the soured cream. Sift the icing sugar into the bowl and beat vigorously until smooth. The texture should be soft and fudgy.

5 Cut the cake in half horizontally and spread a third of the icing in the centre. Replace the top half of the cake and cover the top and sides with icing. Sprinkle over the chopped pistachios and serve in enormous slices!

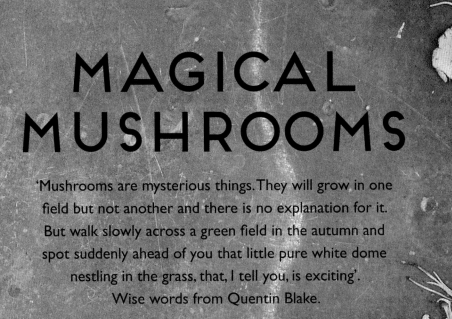

MAGICAL
MUSHROOMS

'Mushrooms are mysterious things. They will grow in one
field but not another and there is no explanation for it.
But walk slowly across a green field in the autumn and
spot suddenly ahead of you that little pure white dome
nestling in the grass, that, I tell you, is exciting'.
Wise words from Quentin Blake.

MUSHROOMS
WITH MISO BROTH AND TOFU

Don't be nervous of tofu; think of it as a gentle ingredient in its own right rather than a substitute for steak. It can be the backdrop for beautifully soft and cleansing recipes – this is a good example. Be generous with the fresh lime, as it really cuts through the seasoning.

MAKES 4 BOWLS – PREP TIME: 15 MINUTES PLUS 10 MINUTES MARINATING
COOK TIME: 15 MINUTES

200g firm tofu, cut into 2cm squares
2 tablespoons soy sauce
2 teaspoons caster sugar
2 teaspoons fish sauce
juice and zest of 1 large unwaxed lime

For the broth
2 teaspoons good-quality vegetable stock granules
1 tablespoon miso paste

3cm piece of ginger, peeled and grated, juices and all
4–5 chestnut mushrooms, thinly sliced
3 spring onions, sliced on the diagonal, keeping some aside, to garnish
300g pre-cooked ribbon noodles (alternatively buy dry noodles and cook according to the instructions)
a bunch of coriander, to garnish

1 Put the tofu into a bowl with the soy sauce, caster sugar, fish sauce and lime juice and zest and leave to marinate for 8–10 minutes.

2 Add 1 litre water to the stock granules and bring to the boil in a large saucepan. Put the miso paste in a small bowl and add a tablespoon or so of the hot vegetable stock. Stir until the miso is liquid and then pour into the large saucepan (this prevents you ending up with a ball of miso paste in the soup).

3 Add the grated ginger to the pot along with any ginger juices that escaped while it was being grated. Tip the mushrooms and spring onions into your soup and simmer, uncovered, for 4–5 minutes.

4 Stir the ribbon noodles into the broth and continue to simmer for a couple of minutes, breaking up the noodles with a spoon. Finally stir through the marinated tofu and all the lovely juices. Gently heat through for 2–3 minutes before serving in bowls. Garnish with fresh coriander.

variation Try udon or glass noodles to replace the ribbon noodles.

MUSHROOM

AND CHESTNUT SOUP

This simple mushroom soup is bolstered with a handful of risotto rice. My husband and I returned to a warming bowl of this after we'd had a freezing swim in the sea – it was exactly what was required to bring us back to life.

SERVES 4 – PREP TIME: 20 MINUTES
COOK TIME: 30 MINUTES

a generous knob of butter
2 tablespoons olive oil
1 garlic clove, crushed
1 onion, chopped
2 celery sticks, chopped
350g mixed wild mushrooms
150ml white wine
100g risotto rice
150g cooked and peeled chestnuts
900ml hot vegetable stock
freshly ground black pepper
4 tablespoons Greek yogurt, to serve

1 Melt the butter in a large saucepan with the olive oil. Add the garlic, onion and celery and sauté for 5 minutes until soft.

2 Add the mushrooms and fry for 3–4 minutes until they have begun to wilt in the heat. Pour over the white wine and increase the heat slightly. Simmer until the liquid has reduced by half before stirring through the rice and chestnuts. Pour over the hot vegetable stock and simmer for 20 minutes.

3 Season the soup really well and purée with a blender or food-processor. Serve immediately in bowls with a lovely dollop of yogurt and a grinding of black pepper.

MUSHROOM

AND GARLIC CARBONARA

We grew up on carbonara once a week and over the years a family recipe was perfected. Each recipe has its nuances and a particular way of cooking this classic, adding garlic or onion, crème fraîche, cream or butter, peas or pancetta. Here I've committed adultery and added mushrooms rather than pancetta but rest assured they make for a totally irresistible dish.

SERVES 2–3 – PREP TIME: 10 MINUTES
COOK TIME: 15 MINUTES

250g dried spaghetti
2 tablespoons olive oil
3 garlic cloves, sliced
300g button mushrooms, sliced in half
2 medium free-range eggs and 1 medium egg yolk
50g Parmesan cheese, finely grated
freshly ground black pepper
a few leaves of rosemary, finely chopped, to garnish

1 Cook the spaghetti in a saucepan with plenty of boiling water for about 8–10 minutes until al dente.

2 Meanwhile, heat the olive oil in a large frying pan over a medium heat and add the garlic and sliced mushrooms. Fry until the steam has subsided and the mushrooms begin to take on a golden tinge, but not a moment longer.

3 In a small bowl, mix together the eggs, egg yolk and plenty of black pepper. Stir in 80 per cent of the Parmesan, keeping the rest for garnish.

4 Drain the spaghetti, reserving a little of the cooking water. Return the spaghetti to the pan and stir through the mushrooms and garlic and then the egg mixture. Stir furiously, then, once it has begun to thicken to a sauce, add a little of the pasta water to loosen the sauce. Continue to mix and quickly empty into warm bowls. Garnish with Parmesan and chopped rosemary and eat immediately.

MUSHROOM
POLPETTE WITH SAGE SPAGHETTI

'Polpette' describes an Italian meatball, but in this instance hearty mushrooms have been used in place of meat. If truth be told, the combination of sage, mushroom and olive oil pasta makes this my favourite recipe in the book.

SERVES 4 – PREP TIME: 20 MINUTES
COOK TIME: 25 MINUTES

For the polpette
3 tablespoons olive oil
3 garlic cloves, crushed
300g chestnut mushrooms, diced
5–6 sage leaves, roughly chopped
a glug of red wine
1 medium free-range egg
40g pecorino cheese, grated
100g fresh white breadcrumbs

300g spaghetti
2 garlic cloves, peeeled and crushed
4–5 sage leaves, finely chopped
a glug of good-quality extra virgin olive oil
a handful of finely grated pecorino
salt and freshly ground black pepper

1 To make the polpette, add just a little of the olive oil to a large, heavy-based frying pan over a medium-high heat. Add the garlic, mushrooms and sage. Fry for 3–4 minutes, until the mushrooms have shrunk and any liquid has been simmered off. Add the wine and continue to fry until it has all but disappeared, leaving behind just the flavour. Season well and transfer the mixture to a bowl to cool slightly.

2 Add the egg, pecorino and breadcrumbs to the bowl and mix together well. With damp hands, shape small spoonfuls of the mixture into balls roughly 40g in weight and about the size of a golf ball. This should make around 12 balls.

3 Bring a large pan of water to the boil for the pasta. Once it has reached a rolling boil, drop in the spaghetti and cook for 8–10 minutes, until al dente.

4 Meanwhile, refocus your attention on the polpette. Return the frying pan to a high heat and add the remaining olive oil. Add the polpette, using tongs, and fry for about 8–10 minutes until golden, resisting the urge to turn them over too often.

5 Drain the spaghetti and return to a gentle heat. Add the garlic, sage and olive oil. Stir to combine. Serve the dish with the polpette balancing on top and top with grated pecorino.

variation *If you aren't able to find pecorino, use a strong Cheddar – this will also work beautifully.*

MUSHROOM

STIR FRY WITH PAK CHOI AND CASHEW NUTS

Once an unaffordable delicacy, dried mushrooms have become easier (and cheaper) to track down. Here, a simple soak in hot water is needed as revitalisation and they are cooked quickly with fresh vegetables, pungent soy and a generous helping of cashew nuts (pictured pages 144-145).

SERVES 4–6 – PREP TIME: 20 MINUTES PLUS 10 MINUTES SOAKING
COOK TIME: 15 MINUTES

45g dried porcini mushrooms
2 shallots, sliced
2 garlic cloves, sliced
1 red chilli, deseeded and finely chopped
1 red pepper, deseeded and finely sliced
¼ green cabbage, shredded
2 pak choi (around 150g), roughly chopped

2 tablespoons sesame oil
75g cashew nuts
1 tablespoon soy sauce

For the coconut sticky rice
1 × 400g can light coconut milk
300g basmati rice

1 Soak the mushrooms in 250ml warm water for 10 minutes. Remove the mushrooms from the water and roughly chop any large ones, saving any precious soaking water. Set aside.

2 Ensure you have prepared the shallots, garlic, chilli, red pepper, cabbage and pak choi, because once you start frying everything comes together quickly.

3 To make the sticky rice, empty the can of coconut milk into a medium saucepan. Now fill the empty can with boiling water and add that to the pot. Finally add the basmati rice. Bring to the boil before simmering for 10 minutes, stirring occasionally. Turn off the heat, cover, and set aside.

4 While the rice is cooking, heat the oil over a medium heat in a wok. Add the shallots and allow them to cook for 2 minutes. Then add the garlic, chilli, red pepper and cashew nuts and leave them to stir-fry for another 2–3 minutes. Add the shredded cabbage and fry for a further couple of minutes. Finish by adding the mushroom liquid, pak choi and soy sauce. Cook for a final 2–3 minutes, until the pak choi has just wilted but retains a lovely, fresh crunch.

5 Serve the stir fry in bowls with a healthy portion of sticky rice.

MUSHROOM
AND STILTON GOUGÈRE

A gougère is a French recipe for savoury baked choux buns. The buns can be giant or tiny and are invariably filled. Here, a choux pastry is spooned around the edge of the dish, which is filled with a gorgeous blue cheese and mushroom filling. The whole lot is baked and the result is a puffy, light, crunchy fence sitting next to a rich and cheesy field of mushrooms.

SERVES 4 – PREP TIME: 40 MINUTES
COOK TIME: 40–45 MINUTES

1 tablespoon olive oil
200g white button mushrooms, sliced
45g unsalted butter
30g plain flour
1 teaspoon dried mustard powder
300ml semi-skimmed milk
75g Stilton cheese, crumbled
small bunch of flat-leaf parsley, leaves
    roughly chopped
a little butter, for greasing

For the cheesy gougère
70g plain flour
¼ teaspoon salt
pinch of cayenne pepper
60g unsalted butter, chopped
2 medium free-range eggs, lightly whisked
45g mature Cheddar cheese, grated

25–30cm shallow ovenproof pie dish

1 To make the filling, heat the oil in a large, deep frying pan, and when hot add the mushrooms. Fry for 6–7 minutes until the steam has died down and the mushrooms are beginning to turn golden. Remove the mushrooms from the pan and set aside.

2 Melt the butter in the pan, then add the flour and mustard powder and mix with a wooden spoon until smooth. Cook for 1 minute. Keep the pan over a low heat and gradually add the milk, a little at a time, stirring constantly to make a smooth sauce. Bring to a simmer and cook for 1 minute. Remove from the heat, add the Stilton, nearly all of the parsley (save a little for garnish) and mushrooms and set aside.

3 Preheat the oven to 220°C/200°C fan/gas mark 7. Lightly grease the dish with a little butter.

4 For the gougère, mix the flour with the salt and cayenne and sift onto a sheet of non-stick parchment paper. Melt the butter with 150ml water and bring to the boil. Pick up the sides of the paper to create a funnel and shoot in the flour (this makes the process extra quick). Remove the pan from the heat and beat vigorously with a wooden spoon for 1 minute, until the mixture is smooth and comes away from the sides of the pan. Set aside.

5 Gradually beat the eggs into the cooled choux mixture, so that it becomes smooth and shiny and rather reluctantly drops off the spoon, then stir in the Cheddar.

6 Spoon the choux mixture in a ring around the edge of the pie dish, pushing it up slightly around the sides. There should be an empty well in the centre for the sauce. Don't panic if it all looks a bit messy and sticky. Spoon your filling into the empty well and bake for 30–35 minutes. Garnish with the remaining parsley and serve immediately, while it is still puffed and beautiful.

MUSHROOM

AND CRÈME FRAICHE TARTS

*A humble tart that suits those enormous mushrooms you often find in farm shops or markets.
The ingredients list is modest, allowing the mushrooms to speak for themselves.*

MAKES 6 TARTS – PREP TIME: 20 MINUTES
COOK TIME: 25 MINUTES

1 tablespoon olive oil
6 large portobello mushrooms, sliced
3 garlic cloves, sliced
sprig of thyme, leaves picked
sprig of rosemary, leaves picked

3 tablespoons balsamic vinegar
375g ready-rolled all-butter puff pastry
6 tablespoons crème fraîche
1 free-range egg, beaten

1 Preheat the oven to 200°C/180°C fan/gas mark 6. Heat the oil in a large frying pan and add the mushrooms, garlic and thyme and rosemary leaves. Fry for 5–6 minutes until the mushrooms have stopped leaking water. Pour in the balsamic vinegar and continue to cook until the balsamic has all but disappeared (the flavour will remain). Set the mushrooms aside.

2 Meanwhile, unroll the pastry and cut into 6 even rectangles. Place on a parchment-lined baking tray and, using a sharp knife, score a 1cm border around the edge of each rectangle, taking care not to cut all the way through.

3 Slather the pastry rectangles with crème fraîche and top with a generous spoonful of the mushroom slices. Brush the edges with the beaten egg and bake in the oven for 15–18 minutes, until puffed up and golden. Serve warm, or cool on a wire rack.

MUSHROOM

BARLEY RISOTTO WITH MASCARPONE AND HERBS

Barley risotto is slightly different from its white counterpart. As well as impressing health conscious guests with countless nutritional benefits, pearl barley offers an unusual, nutty texture that goes particularly well with the mushrooms' rich, dark flavour. This is a perfect winter recipe, ideal for bleak days when the sun has set too early.

SERVES 3–4 – PREP TIME: 20 MINUTES
COOK TIME: 45–50 MINUTES

2 tablespoons olive oil
250g mushrooms (enoki, chanterelle or chestnut),
    gently washed and sliced
a knob of butter
4 garlic cloves, sliced
a few sprigs of fresh thyme
1 small onion, finely chopped

175g pearl barley
750ml hot vegetable stock
2 tablespoons mascarpone
a grating of Parmesan cheese
freshly ground black pepper
a handful of fresh herbs (parsley, chervil or chives),
    to garnish

1 Heat a little of the olive oil in a large, deep frying pan. Add the mushrooms and fry for 2–3 minutes over a high heat until they have lost a little of their structure. Remove the mushrooms from the pan and set aside on a plate.

2 Add the knob of butter to the frying pan and, once bubbling, add the garlic, thyme and onion. Reduce the heat to medium and continue to fry for a few minutes until the onion has softened, but not coloured.

3 Stir the pearl barley through the buttery onion mixture and pour over the hot stock. Leave to simmer, stirring occasionally, for about 30–35 minutes, until the barley is soft but still has a little bite in the centre. If the pan runs dry, add a little more water.

4 Once the barley is cooked, return the mushrooms to the pan with the mascarpone and Parmesan, and season with a little black pepper. Serve in hot bowls, garnished with a scattering of fresh herbs.

tip! *Use any leftover risotto to stuff into mushrooms, tomatoes or peppers for a wholesome lunch.*

CABBAGES & KINGS

'The time has come, the Walrus said, To talk of many things: Of shoes and ships and sealing-wax, Of cabbages and kings...'

Although shoes, ships and sealing wax are hopefully rarely seen on ingredients lists, cabbages, along with the other brassicas in this chapter, are certainly kings of the table. The beautiful combination of leaves and flowers, crunch and chew, gives this regal collection of greenery bite and flavour fit for a king.

CHARRED
ROMANESCO
WITH BUTTERED ALMONDS AND GARLIC

Romanesco is a spectacular vegetable – its spiralling shape and beautifully soft green palette immediately catches your attention. The gently cooked florets' lovely flavour is complemented by the crunch of buttered, salted almonds. Toss through brown rice or throw into a simple risotto to transform this dish into a main meal.

SERVES 4 AS A SIDE DISH – PREP TIME: 10 MINUTES
COOK TIME: 10 MINUTES

1 head of Romanesco broccoli
a large knob of butter
75g whole blanched almonds, halved

3 garlic cloves, roughly chopped
½ teaspoon sea salt

1 Remove the stem of the Romanesco, cutting around the core and then trimming the florets from the inner stem. Bring a large pan of water to the boil and add the Romanesco florets. Simmer for 5–6 minutes, until just cooked through but with a little bite.

2 Heat the butter in a large frying pan over a low-medium heat and add the almonds and garlic. Fry until they have begun to take on some colour, for about 2–3 minutes. Sprinkle over the sea salt.

3 Drain the Romanesco and empty into the garlic and almond butter. Toss to combine and season well. Serve immediately.

CAULIFLOWER

AND CHICKPEA YELLOW CURRY

My husband became a vegetarian during the course of writing this book because he rated and scored most of the hundred recipes. Samples would arrive fresh from the kitchen and he would sit and cast judgement. This curry was his favourite. I'd say that was a strong recommendation. Switch the green chillies for red if you like your curries to be hot.

SERVES 4 – PREP TIME: 15 MINUTES
COOK TIME: 30 MINUTES

75g cashew nuts
about 1 tablespoon vegetable oil
1 large onion, roughly chopped
2 green chillies, sliced in half lengthways
   and finely sliced
4 garlic cloves, finely chopped
5–6cm piece of ginger, peeled and grated
1 teaspoon curry powder
1 teaspoon turmeric

1 large head of cauliflower (around 600g),
   divided into florets
1 × 400g can chickpeas, rinsed and drained
400ml coconut milk
1 teaspoon nigella seeds
100g young leaf spinach
30g bunch coriander, roughly chopped
salt and freshly ground black pepper

1 Heat a deep frying pan over a medium heat. Add the cashews and 'dry-fry' them for 3–4 minutes, shaking the pan occasionally, until a lovely nutty aroma starts to linger and the nuts become a little charred. Remove from the pan and set aside.

2 Return the pan to the heat and add the oil. Once hot, add the onion and cook for 2–3 minutes until beginning to caramelise. Add the green chilli, garlic, ginger, curry powder and turmeric, pouring in another glug of olive oil if needed. Continue to fry until the onions are soft and the chillies have lost their vibrancy.

3 Add the cauliflower florets, chickpeas and coconut milk into the pan and give everything a good stir. Tip in the cashew nuts and nigella seeds. Bring to a simmer and cook, covered, for 20 minutes until the sauce has begun to thicken.

4 Stir through the spinach and 2–3 tablespoons water if the sauce is looking a little thick. Season well. Replace the lid for a couple of moments until the spinach has just wilted. Stir through half the chopped coriander, stalks and all. Serve, garnished with a little more chopped coriander.

GREEN

CABBAGE

BUTTERMILK COLESLAW WITH MACADAMIAS

The addition of buttermilk to this coleslaw lifts the dressing, moving it from a cloggy, store-bought affair to something light and really interesting. Don't be afraid to add a little more carrot or a little less cabbage. Make it your own and serve it with pride.

SERVES 6–8 – PREP TIME: 25 MINUTES
COOK TIME: 5 MINUTES

a knob of butter
100g macadamia nuts,
   roughly chopped
1 head of small green
   cabbage (about 600g)
a large bunch of flat-leaf
   parsley, leaves chopped
2 medium carrots, grated
3 spring onions, finely
   chopped

salt and freshly ground
   black pepper

For the dressing
75g mayonnaise
125ml buttermilk
1 teaspoon cider vinegar
½ teaspoon sea salt
pinch of cayenne pepper
¼ teaspoon mustard
   powder

1 Make the dressing by putting the mayonnaise into a small bowl and slowly adding the buttermilk, mixing well as you go to prevent any lumps. Stir through the cider vinegar, salt, cayenne and mustard powder. Set aside.

2 Heat the butter in a small frying pan over a medium heat. Add the macadamia nuts and toast for 3–4 minutes, paying careful attention to prevent them burning. Remove the pan from the heat and set aside.

3 Shred the cabbage as fine as your knife skills will allow. Transfer to a huge bowl with the parsley, carrots and spring onions, then add half the toasted nuts. Pour in the dressing and mix well, adding a little more cayenne if you want to increase the heat. Season well with salt and black pepper. Tip the coleslaw into your serving bowl and garnish with the remaining macadamia nuts.

tip! *This dish can be made up to a day before it's needed, just add a little fresh parsley before it hits the table.*

BRUSSELS SPROUTS

CHEDDAR AND LEMON SALAD

Brussels are the vegetable equivalent of the kid who is picked last in the playground. They sit there, in their net sacks waiting to be chosen and only get the go-ahead for the festive Yuletide outing. Well, I've mixed things up a little and served them raw, tossed with Cheddar, lemon and raisins and the result makes them stand out from the line-up.

SERVES 4 AS A SIDE – PREP TIME: 20 MINUTES

300g Brussels sprouts
   (see method)
zest of 1 large unwaxed
   lemon
60g mature Cheddar
   cheese, finely grated
100g plump raisins

For the dressing
juice of 1 large lemon
2 tablespoons extra
   virgin olive oil

1 The bulk of the prep for this recipe is chopping the sprouts. Use a sharp knife and get into a rhythm. Remove the stalk and any tough outer leaves. Slice each in half vertically and then shred the sprouts as finely as your knife skills allow.

2 Add the lemon zest to the sprouts, along with the grated Cheddar cheese and raisins. Combine well.

3 Make the dressing by mixing the lemon juice and olive oil in a small bowl. Pour the dressing over the sprouts mixture until the salad is evenly dressed. Serve.

ASIAN SLAW

'You are what you eat.' We've all heard this mantra before and this salad makes you feel good. The lime, mint and fish sauce all sit together beautifully but it's the crunch of the salted peanuts that really finishes it off. Take on a picnic as a lovely alternative to a heavy sandwich.

SERVES 6 – PREP TIME: 10 MINUTES
COOK TIME: 5 MINUTES

120g vermicelli noodles (also known as
   glass noodles)
½ head sweetheart cabbage, finely sliced
¼ small head red cabbage, finely sliced
60g mangetout, sliced on the diagonal
1 large green chilli, deseeded and finely chopped
6 small spring onions, finely sliced
a large bunch of mint, roughly chopped, keeping
   a few leaves whole to garnish

150g salted, roasted peanuts, roughly chopped,
   keeping a few whole to garnish

For the dressing
2 garlic cloves, finely chopped
2 tablespoons fish sauce
1 tablespoon caster sugar
juice and zest of 2 unwaxed limes

1 Empty the dry noodles into a medium bowl and pour over boiling water until they are completely covered. Leave to soak for 3–5 minutes or until just tender. Drain and run under cool water until the noodles are separated. A good trick is then to take scissors to your noodles, cutting them into shorter lengths; this makes the noodles a little more manageable to eat.

2 Meanwhile, make your dressing by combining all the ingredients. Allow it to sit for a few minutes, if you have the time. The garlic will infuse with the lime juice and it will taste all the better.

3 The next step is super simple. Put all the ingredients in a large bowl. Pour over the dressing and use a 'lifting' motion to make sure the whole salad is dressed.

4 Serve with fresh mint and a few peanuts sprinkled on top.

CABBAGE

LEAVES WITH SUN-DRIED TOMATO RISOTTO

There is something very beautiful about the intricately wrinkled leaves of a Savoy cabbage; they seem wiser and more interesting than their white contemporaries and wouldn't be seen dead in a coleslaw. I wanted to use the leaves and play with them a little. Their fate was to be stuffed with an almost sweet tomato risotto and laid to rest in a pool of white wine sauce. This is a great recipe to prepare ahead of time; make the risotto and leave to cool and blanch the cabbage leaves and then assemble later.

SERVES 4 – PREP TIME: 10 MINUTES
COOK TIME: 50 MINUTES

8 large outer leaves of a Savoy cabbage
fresh green salad, to serve

For the risotto
1 tablespoon olive oil
1 onion, finely sliced
200g risotto rice (Arborio or Carnaroli)
800ml very hot chicken stock
2 tablespoons red pesto

100g sun-dried tomatoes, roughly chopped
salt and freshly ground black pepper

For the sauce
a knob of butter
2 shallots, finely chopped
150ml white wine
200ml double cream

1 To make the risotto, heat the oil in a deep sauté pan over a high heat. Add the onion and fry for 2–3 minutes until it turns translucent and edging towards golden.

2 Over a gentle heat, add the risotto rice to the pan and stir so the grains are coated in oil. Gradually add all the hot stock, one ladleful at a time, stirring until each addition is absorbed before adding the next – this will take about 20 minutes, so go slowly. Season.

3 When the risotto is cooked and the stock has been absorbed, stir through the pesto and sun-dried tomatoes.

4 Preheat the oven to 180°C/160°C fan/gas mark 4. Select the outer 8 leaves of the cabbage (no more as the inner leaves are too small) and cut away a triangle section of the thick base end. Blanch the leaves in batches in a large pan of boiling water for a minute or so, until softened but not boiled; remove and leave to cool.

5 Once the risotto and leaves are cool, make the parcels; divide the risotto into 8 and using a spoon add a portion to the bottom of each leaf. Roll the leaves up, one at a time, tucking the sides in as you go and placing the parcels into an ovenproof dish with the seam side down so they have no chance to unwrap.

6 Make the white sauce by melting the butter in a small pan over a medium heat. Add the shallots and fry until they soften but don't colour. Pour over the wine and increase the heat a little. Allow it to bubble for around 5 minutes until halved in volume, then pour over the cream. Reduce the heat and simmer for a minute or so.

7 Pour the creamy sauce over your cabbage rolls and give the dish a good grating of black pepper. Bake in the oven for 20 minutes before serving with a fresh green salad.

KALE

AND QUINOA WITH WALNUT LABNEH BALLS

Labneh is yogurt that has been strained in muslin to remove the whey, giving it a consistency between yogurt and soft cheese, while retaining the yogurt's distinctive sour taste. We served labneh balls, rolled in nuts and herbs, as part of a Middle Eastern sharing feast at my latest pop-up restaurant and they were so enthusiastically received, I decided to use them here. It is worth making the labneh balls two or three days in advance.

SERVES 4 – PREP TIME: 30 MINUTES (PLUS 2 DAYS FOR THE LABNEH BALLS TO FORM)
COOK TIME: 30 MINUTES

For the labneh balls
500g good-quality yogurt, 10% fat if possible
125g walnuts
2 rosemary sprigs, leaves picked
1 teaspoon sweet paprika

For the quinoa
200g quinoa
600ml hot vegetable stock

juice of ½ lemon
100g kale
50g sultanas

For the dressing
2 large garlic cloves, crushed
3 tablespoons sesame tahini
1 tablespoon lemon juice

1 To make the labneh, lay a piece of muslin in the bottom of a sieve and add the yogurt. Gather the edges of the cloth, enclosing the yogurt, and place the sieve over a bowl. Leave in the fridge and allow to drain for 2 days. After this time, gently squeeze out any excess liquid and open the muslin to reveal your labneh cheese. Now you simply shape the mixture into small balls, each roughly 20g in weight. The balls can be stored for 2 weeks covered in olive oil or eaten immediately.

2 Heat a medium frying pan over a high heat. Add the walnuts and toast for 3–4 minutes, tossing the pan frequently. Remove from the heat and very finely chop 75g of the walnuts and the picked rosemary leaves.

3 Return the frying pan to the heat and add the dry quinoa, over a medium heat. You will now begin to hear the tiny grains popping – move the pan frequently so the grains toast evenly. After 5 minutes or so, the popping will slow down. Pour the hot stock over the quinoa, cover

and simmer for 15 minutes until the grains are plump and cooked through. Squeeze over the lemon juice.

4 Meanwhile, bring a large pan of salted water to the boil. Add the kale and blanch for 2 minutes over a high heat. Drain, allow to cool and squeeze out any excess water with your hands. Coarsely chop the kale and add it to the cooked quinoa with the sultanas and remaining walnuts.

5 To make the dressing, combine all the ingredients in a small bowl or jam jar with around 75ml warm water – you need enough warm water to create a pouring consistency.

6 Roll your labne balls in the chopped walnuts and rosemary and sprinkle over the paprika. Serve on top of the quinoa with the dressing on the side.

tip! If you don't have time to make your own labneh balls, try gently moulding balls of cream cheese and coating them with chopped toasted walnuts.

COCONUT NOODLES WITH

CHINESE CABBAGE

AND SPRING ONION

My blog, 'Fuggle Antics' has been a labour of love for five years, a journey and diary of my life with food. It has prompted cyber-relationships with fellow cooks across the globe and culinary experiences that I may never have thought possible, but mostly it has encouraged me to eat adventurously. Discovering ramen noodle bars has been one of those adventures. Ramen is a noodle dish with rich stock and springy noodles at the core. This recipe is my 'do at home' version. It is important to keep tasting the broth until you are happy, adding a little more spice or a dash of coconut milk as you feel necessary.

MAKES 4 LARGE BOWLS – PREP TIME: 20 MINUTES
COOK TIME: 20 MINUTES

2 large free-range eggs
1 tablespoon sesame oil
2 small shallots, finely chopped
2 small green chillies, deseeded and finely chopped
2 tablespoons thick red Thai curry paste
½ tablespoon brown sugar
½ tablespoon fish sauce

400g udon noodles, ready cooked
400g Chinese cabbage, finely chopped
400ml coconut milk (use the light or normal version)
75g salted peanuts, roughly chopped, to garnish
fresh coriander, roughly chopped, to garnish

1 Soft boil your eggs by heating a medium saucepan of water until simmering and add the eggs. Set the timer for 7 minutes.

2 Meanwhile, heat a frying pan and add the sesame oil. Allow the oil to get perfectly hot before adding the shallot, and chillies. Fry for a minute or two before stirring through the red curry paste, brown sugar and fish sauce. There should be a delicious fragrance in your kitchen at this point. Allow the mixture to gently bubble for 1–2 minutes.

3 Using a slotted spoon, remove the eggs from the water and set aside. Add the udon noodles and cabbage to the egg water and cover and simmer for 2–3 minutes. Remove the lid and drain, returning the cabbage and noodles to the empty pan while you finish the sauce.

4 Stir the coconut milk and 400ml water into your spice paste and allow to simmer for 7–8 minutes, stirring occasionally.

5 Peel the shell from the eggs and cut them in half. Using tongs, place the noodles and cabbage in the bottom of 4 bowls and ladle over the hot coconut sauce. Finish with half an egg, chopped peanuts and fresh coriander. Serve immediately with chopsticks or forks (depending on the crowd).

tip! Ramen and udon noodles are easily available from supermarkets.

CAVOLO NERO

AND PARMESAN BAKED EGGS

Sunday evenings are often about eggs in my house, with many variations depending on the day or the season. My husband would opt for poached, my son, scrambled, but I will always choose baked eggs. There is something cute about each having your own little pot, a tiny meal, just enough to satisfy. This variation has become one of my best, it looks beautiful and the addition of pan-fried garlic and cavolo finish it off perfectly.

MAKES 4 RAMEKINS – PREP TIME: 5 MINUTES
COOK TIME: 30 MINUTES

15g butter, plus a little for greasing
8–10 long stems of cavolo nero
2 garlic cloves, crushed
150ml double cream
4 large free-range eggs

a little sprinkling of Parmesan cheese
sea salt flakes and freshly ground black pepper
buttered soldiers, to serve

4 × 250ml ramekins

1 Preheat the oven to 180°C/160°C fan/gas mark 4. Lightly butter the inside of the ramekins.

2 Prepare the cavolo nero by cutting the leaves free from the stalks and roughly chopping the leaves into 2–3cm strips. Discard the stalks.

3 Place a large, wide frying pan over a medium heat and melt the butter. Add the cavolo nero strips and garlic, then season with sea salt and pepper. Stir and cook the cavolo nero for 5–6 minutes until wilted and add the cream. Bubble for 3–4 minutes, or until thickened. Season generously.

4 Spoon the mixture into the bottom of 4 ramekins and crack an egg on top of each. Sprinkle over the Parmesan. Transfer the ramekins to a roasting tin and fill the tin with boiling water until it reaches half way up the ramekins – this creates a lovely steamy environment for the eggs so there is no chance of them drying out as they cook. Carefully transfer the tin to the oven and bake the eggs for 15–20 minutes. Serve with buttered soldiers.

CAVOLO NERO

WITH SOBA NOODLES, LIME AND TAMARIND

Delicate and beautiful, these noodles are tossed with a sweet ginger dressing and pepped with lime. I've added plenty of blanched cavolo nero and bright avocado for good measure. Sometimes I like to eat this with extra soy for a salty edge (pictured pages 166–7).

SERVES 4 – PREP TIME: 15 MINUTES
COOK TIME: 10 MINUTES

250g soba noodles
1 head of cavolo nero (about 200g)
1 ripe avocado
4 spring onions, sliced
40g sesame seeds, to garnish

For the dressing
1–2 garlic cloves, crushed
1 teaspoon tamarind paste
4cm piece of ginger, peeled and finely grated
1 tablespoon maple syrup
2 tablespoons extra virgin olive oil
2 teaspoons sesame oil
finely grated zest and juice of 1 unwaxed lime

1 Cook the soba noodles by adding them to boiling water and simmering, according to the pack instructions, usually for about 5 minutes. Drain and rinse well under running water until cool.

2 Meanwhile, separate the cavolo nero leaves and then trim the tough base of each. Roughly chop them and cook in a pan of lightly salted boiling water for 3–4 minutes, until tender. Cool and drain well then squeeze out any excess water and roughly chop.

3 Make the dressing by putting all the ingredients (including any ginger juice) into a jar and mix well until combined.

4 Cut the avocado flesh into 2cm chunks and set aside.

5 Put the noodles and cavolo nero into a large bowl and pour over the dressing. Combine thoroughly before carefully mixing through the avocado and spring onion; a light touch will mean the avocado doesn't turn to mush.

6 Serve on plates sprinkled with sesame seeds.

KALE

AND BLACK OLIVE TAGLIATELLE

I love lazy days with little on the agenda, a gentle pace of life with simple food and lovely friends. This tagliatelle is for those days; it takes moments to put together and can sit in the centre of your table with no frills required.

SERVES 2–3 – PREP TIME: 10 MINUTES
COOK TIME: 12 MINUTES

75g curly leaf kale, large stalks removed and leaves
   roughly shredded
250g fresh tagliatelle
80g black olives, pitted and halved

2 tablespoons olive oil
2 large free-range egg yolks, beaten
plenty of salt and freshly ground black pepper

1 Bring a large pan of water to the boil and drop in the kale. Simmer for 3–4 minutes before removing the kale from the pan with a large draining spoon or tongs. Set the blanched kale aside for a few minutes while you cook the pasta in the same water.

2 Make sure the water returns to a simmer before adding the fresh tagliatelle. Simmer for 3–4 minutes until the pasta is just cooked. Working quickly, drain and return the pasta to the pan, along with the kale. Add the black olives, olive oil and heaps of seasoning.

3 Once you are ready to serve, pour the egg yolks into the pasta and gently toss the pasta, allowing the eggs to cook in the residual heat. That's it. Serve immediately.

BROCCOLI

WITH BULGAR, DRIED CHERRIES AND PISTACHIO

Broccoli should be given more attention. Florets are so often forced to sit on the side of a plate, lacking luster and boiled beyond recognition, but this should not be their destiny. With careful cooking and a few sophisticated ingredients — tart dried cherries, bulgur wheat and pistachio nuts — the broccoli steps up and tastes unrecognisably chic.

SERVES 3 – PREP TIME: 15 MINUTES
COOK TIME: 20 MINUTES

a healthy sized head of broccoli, divided
   into florets
2 tablespoons olive oil
150g bulgar wheat
50g dried cherries, plus a few to garnish
50g pistachios, roughly chopped
zest of 1 unwaxed lemon

For the dressing
3 tablespoons Greek yogurt
2 tablespoons red wine vinegar
1 tablespoon extra virgin olive oil
salt and freshly ground black pepper

1 Preheat the oven to 180°C/160°C fan/gas mark 4. Spread the broccoli florets out on a tray and drizzle them well with olive oil. Put them in the oven to roast for 20 minutes.

2 Meanwhile make your bulgar wheat by tipping it into a large bowl and seasoning. Pour over 150ml boiling water. Cover the bowl with clingfilm and allow it to sit for 10 minutes. Remove the clingfilm, fluff the bulgar wheat up with a fork and stir through the dried cherries, pistachios, lemon zest and roasted broccoli.

3 To make the dressing, mix all the dressing ingredients together with a dash of hot water. Pour the dressing over the salad and gently toss until well combined. Serve in one, two or three bowls garnished with a few extra dried cherries. Serve immediately.

INDEX

INDEX

THANK YOU'S

Writing this book has been a journey. There have been lots of moments when I've metaphorically sped along costal roads, not another car in sight and loved the experience. The were other times that I needed the guidance and support of my amazing team and I'm so thankful for them.

It isn't every book that gets put together by lovely colleagues that I now very much consider my friends. Sophie and Nicky have serious vision and I love that they are brave and creative. Thank you for all the hard work you've both put in.

Tori, who shot the book, has been a friend since the age of 13. Together, we went to our first nightclub, caught our first flight without our parents and explored festivals as young free things. Together, we've created this book and I'm so grateful for her. May there be many more adventures.

My Jasper who, aged two, has sat on my kitchen surface watching me cook and frequently, unashamedly, commented on the success of the recipes. He has become practiced at grinding the pepper mill and very, very fast stirring.

Nick keeps me on my toes and encourages me to whistle while I work. Our home became a vegetarian sanctuary for a year and he's rarely grumbled at eating more lentils than I'm sure most thirty-something boys might. We've had adventures to markets, eaten at vegetarian restaurants and hosted friends to dinner, all in aid of creating this collection. Thank you for being my sidekick.

And one more thank you. To my family; Caroline, Milla, Calandre, Oenone, Hannah, Lou, Sue and my Mum who have tested recipes throughout the year, dropping anything to help and not been scared to give feedback. Thank you.